The Cardiac Kids
A Season to Remember

by
Bill Murphy

Pen & Publish

Published by Pen & Publish
Bloomington, Indiana
(812) 837-9226
info@PenandPublish.com
www.PenandPublish.com

ISBN-13: 978-0-9800429-0-0 ISBN-10: 0-9800429-0-9
This book is printed on acid free paper.

Printed in the USA

Front Cover: Rose Bowl Program Courtesy: Tournament of Roses Archives.
Back Cover: Indiana University Archives

Dedication

To Wanda, Ryan, & Kate, without your love and support, everything else is meaningless.
To my parents for all you have done.
To the team who made those Saturdays so special.
To my Grandmother Murphy, thank you.

Acknowledgements

I am forever indebted to the members of the '67 IU football team for their cooperation with this book. They gave so freely of their time, their pictures, and their stories. I was a junior high student when this season took place, and these gentlemen were my heroes. After this endeavor, I can truly say they are men of the highest character. I was deeply moved by their compassion with me and my many requests, how they cared about each other, and how they truly were indeed one big very special family with a patriarch in Coach John Pont who could not have been more gracious with his time.

I would like to thank Brad Cook and Dina Kellams of the Indiana University Archives for sharing pictures of the season and Bob Hammel for his stories.

I thank the Indiana University football team, Coach Lynch, and especially B. J. Ferrand for all their help with this project.

On a personal note, I would like to thank my parents who took me to the games so very long ago. I would like to thank my two children, now adults, Ryan and Kate, for their support and inspiration with this project. A special thanks to my best friend, my partner in life, my wife, Wanda, without whose help this book would not have been possible. Finally, a special thanks goes to the memory of my late Grandmother Murphy who provided the tickets and the many articles of research for this book. For as long as I can remember, we would go to her house to pick up the tickets before the game, and after the game we would go back to eat and visit. There waiting for me in the corner, were newspapers, sometimes stacked a couple feet high, waiting for me to take home. Those papers seemed like Christmas presents all fall and winter, and I took great care and delight in reading them over and over.

I hope in reading this book, you can enjoy with me this special season over and over again, as I have done the past forty years. Someone once asked me, when did you start this book, and I can honestly answer forty years ago at Second Street in Bloomington. The '67 season was very special, the coaches were special, and the players were special. Will it happen again? I think so. I hope so, and

I, like many of you, will be there rooting the Hoosiers on. But for now, please feel free to root on the '67 team as you read A Season to Remember, as the Cardiac Kids once more grace the gridiron with the daring of a bandit at Fort Knox. GO HOOSIERS!

Table of Contents

Chapter 1	The Making of the Team	1
Chapter 2	Indiana vs. Kentucky; The Beginning	5
Chapter 3	Indiana vs. Kansas; The Battle of the Substitute Kickers	13
Chapter 4	Indiana vs. Illinois; The Defense Stars	19
Chapter 5	Indiana vs. Iowa; Gambling Harry	25
Chapter 6	Indiana vs. Michigan; Punt John, Punt	35
Chapter 7	Indiana vs. Arizona; Jade's Night to Shine	41
Chapter 8	Indiana vs. Wisconsin; Homecoming	45
Chapter 9	Indiana vs. Michigan State; Duffy's Revenge	53
Chapter 10	Indiana vs. Minnesota; A Half Step Off	59
Chapter 11	Preparing for Purdue	65
Chapter 12	Indiana vs. Purdue; The Ultimate Bucket Game	69
Chapter 13	Terry Hoeppner; A Rose Bowl Wish	81
Chapter 14	California Here We Come	83
Chapter 15	Pre-Rose Bowl	87
Chapter 16	Indiana vs. University of Southern California; The Rose Bowl	91
Chapter 17	Notes on the Season	101
Chapter 18	Terry Cole; "T-Bear"	109
Chapter 19	Doug Crusan; "The Captain"	111
Chapter 20	Harry Gonso; "The Field General"	113
Chapter 21	Jade Butcher; "The Knothole Kid"	115
Chapter 22	Harold Mauro; "The Monk"	117
Chapter 23	Ken Kaczmarek; "Kaz"	119
Chapter 24	John Isenbarger; "The Cardiac Kid"	121
Chapter 25	John Pont; "Coach"	123
Chapter 26	Players of '67	125
Chapter 27	Honors of the '67 Hoosiers	131
	About the Auther	135
	Bibliograpgy	137

Chapter 1

The Making of the Team

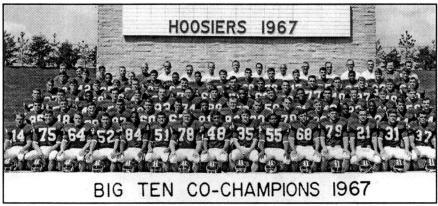

Indiana University Archives

After 40 years of wins, losses, blood, sweat, and general athletic fever, there is one team in all of IU football history that

Indiana University Archives
(966-0225.2)

holds a special place in every Hoosier's heart. This is their story.....

Coach Pont speaks with pride of the team picture he still has in his den. He calls it a great photo, "It is a great photo because everyone was at attention, they had a good sharp look in their faces. No one Mickey Moused around or anything like that. I looked at the picture and said this is going to be a great football team, and it was."

Pont reminisced about where it all started, "We as a coaching staff decided that in Gonso, Isenbarger, Butcher, and Eric Stolberg, we had a group of very

1

quick, athletically skilled players who were not necessarily big or fast but very, very, quick. After looking at our offense following the '66 season, we made a decision to change both the offense and defense. We had practiced the I formation at Yale. We knew the I formation was new to the Big Ten, and in fact we were the first team to use it, and we were also the first team to use a 4-4 defense in the Big Ten as well."

"The first thing we told everyone was that they were going to have to lose weight. After practice in the fall, I called John Isenbarger in first, and we told John that we were going to go with Harry at the quarterback spot and move him to tailback and he accepted it." "We had talked to Doug Crusan in the spring, and told him that we needed his size on defense because although Jerry Grecco and Billy Wolfe were very quick, they were not big and we knew we needed more size on defense. I told him that I knew he was thinking about professional football, but we wanted him to try defense, and he said ok for the sake of the team. We then called in Terry Cole and said that we were going to go with the I formation and we wanted him to be the fullback, but that he wasn't going to carry the ball much. In fact, there would be games when he would only carry the ball 2 or 3 times a game, but that we needed his size and speed as a blocker. Terry replied very quickly saying coach in that high pitched voice of his, I don't care, I just want to win and he accepted his role quickly and with great determination. By now, a number of personnel decisions had been made on both our offense and defense."

"The offensive line was not big, but they were extremely quick. Al Gage, who played tight-end at 195 lbs., was very quick off the ball, and with tackles, Bob Kirk, and Richard Spickard, guards, Russell, and Cassells, and Mauro at center, we were very quick along the line. We just kept telling the players, you are going to lose weight because we are going to be a quick sprint out and option team, and it just fit our personnel beautifully. Our defense was made up of older guys, Doug was our Captain. The defense, made up mostly of juniors and seniors, were very talented athletes who took an active roll of leadership, and everything just blended together perfectly. This would enable us to be the first school in the Big Ten to use the I formation and go with a sprint out attack."

There were two things that brought this team together. The first took place after the doubles sessions had just about finished. Pont recalled, "We were eating together one night, and I called on one of the trainers, a student named Dean Kleinschmidt, a very creative student, and asked him to come up with some way to break the tensions of doubles and relax the team. Well, Dean gets everyone's attention and says we're going to sing a song. He started and everyone was quiet, they just didn't know what to do. Dean gets on a chair and starts singing his version of We've Got the Whole World in Our Hands. He starts with we've got the best offense in the land, and then he went to the defense, to the coaches, then he went to each position and he kept singing we've got the best in the land. He went through them all and by now the entire team was standing on their chairs, tables and singing." Pont paused, and said, "It was a moment to be captured." This song became the theme song for the team for the entire season. Right then and there, the coaching staff knew that they had a good football team because this had brought everyone together.

The second incident that evolved in the making of this team was a result of a cookout for the team. Darrell and Eddie French were close friends of Ponts and they owned Mechanic's Laundry in Bloomington. They did a lot of entertaining at their lake house at Geist, which Pont said was a big place, "just huge". Pont asked Darrell if his dad would ever host the entire football team, trainers and families. Ed Sr. was asked and he said sure we can do it. "So after doubles, we took the team, girlfriends, wives, coaches, and their wives up to Geist, and I told the players you can do whatever you want to do, you can swim, play basketball, tennis, do it all, then they are going to feed you and it will be steak, it will be shrimp, the whole thing. We arrived as a team going down the stairway to the main level. As the players started down, the pep band started playing the Indiana Fight Song. The stairs and the main level were decorated in red and white, the players couldn't believe what they were seeing. The players played, had fun, ate a huge meal and at eight o'clock that evening, the players got back on the bus to Bloomington with instructions from the coaching staff that they would see them on Sunday." In the eyes of Coach Pont, those two events were the start of the making of the '67 Hoosiers and the magical season that would transpire.

The words, chemistry, courage, sacrifice, respect, and love were all words both uttered and demonstrated by the players as they talked about what made this team so special. Gonso said, " It was a combination of the chemistry of the individuals that made up the team that made this team so special, really a combination of the older seniors who were solid, stable, great athletes with the spark of some young sophomores who did not know their own limitations. It took people by surprise. Not only was it Indiana being a new force, but a new style of offense and combined with a quick aggressive defense that people had not seen before."

The players truly admired and respected each other as witnessed in the remarks made about the various games throughout the season. Harold Mauro recalling both the Michigan and Michigan State away games, remarked, "Thank God for John Isenbarger, he won those games for us." Jade Butcher recalled the coaching staff, pointing out Harold Mauro blocking again and again at film sessions, and with a huge smile recalled his friend Terry Cole having a career game against Purdue. Butcher said, "I looked around on Terry's 63 yard TD run and was going to block for him, when I realized he was already ahead of me and wide open to the end zone." Gonso recalled Butcher as a gifted and special receiver saying, "They just don't make players like Jade anymore." John Isenbarger chocked with emotion about Terry Cole and the contributions he made to this team. Then there was Ken Kaczmarek on a June night nearly 40 years later making sure that the night would be perfect for his teammates joining him in the Indiana Football Hall of Fame. The offensive stars talking about the defense saying they were truly the backbone of the team. Jade Butcher saying that, "After the Illinois game, we knew our defense wasn't just good, but truly great."

In talking with these players, it was easy to see what made this team and season so special. It wasn't just the wins or the trip to the Rose Bowl, it was the fact that this team was indeed a family, and the season that followed would be a season to be placed in a family photo album of memories for all time, a football season for all seasons.

Chapter 2

Indiana vs. Kentucky
September 23, 1967

The Beginning

*Captain Doug Crusan leads the Hoosiers
on the field to start the season.
Indiana University Archives (67-1229.1)*

The magical season of '67 started on a beautiful fall day, Sept. 23, 1967. The sun shone brightly as Indiana prepared to open the season with the Wildcats of the University of Kentucky. Fans arriving to Memorial Stadium could check the back of their game day program to find out that the '68 Chevrolets were dramatic, distinctive, and daringly new, much like the '67 Hoosier football team. The students could go to the Indiana Theatre to see Robert Wagner and Jill St. John starring in The Banning, or go to the Princess and see Ursula Andress, Peter Sellers, David Niven and Orson Wells in Casino Royal, which according to the advertisement, was too much for one James Bond.

September 23, 1967 I.U. Stadium

On this day, the game day program featured Terry Cole, Nate Cunningham, and Gary Cassells in the Hoosier Profiles, which proved to be prophetic for the huge roll each would play as the season unfolded. Before each home game, fans could enjoy a luncheon in the new fieldhouse, served from 11:00 A.M. until game time, catered by the Indiana Memorial Union.

The game day crowd could buy their program for $.49, wave an IU pennant for $1.00, and boast of their team spirit with a $.25

button. Hungry fans could feast on $.40 hamburgers, $.30 hot dogs, popcorn and peanuts for $.15 each, while washing it all down with a $.15 soft drink. Ironically, on page 14 of the program, Ellis Floral Shop's add featured a rose, although there was no mention of Jan. 1, to be found anywhere.

The game started at 1:30 p.m. and the IU officials warned everyone to arrive early to avoid the traffic. This would be the first meeting of the neighboring state universities since 1927. The two schools were set to meet six times in the next eight years. IU had won four of the first seven games that included one tie. However, Kentucky would enter this game as a three point favorite.

IU's new dimension was a potential outside running game which had been missing in Coach John Pont's first two seasons, during which time his Hoosiers had won 3, lost 16, and tied one. Previously, IU had relied on drop back passes and an inside power game, whereas on the '67 team, they would rely more on their team speed and an outside running game.

Indiana had spent the summer working on a weight reduction program designed to improve team speed and quickness. The results seemed to show the program's worth, as the previous spring only 13 Hoosiers could break five seconds in the 40-yard dash, and on the first day of fall practice in this new season, there were 27 players to record speeds of 5 seconds and under.

Kentucky under the leadership of Coach Charley Bradshaw, came into the game like IU, relying heavily on sophomores with an offense built around former defensive back, Dicky Lyons, who was switched to tailback. The game marked the first time IU had played a Southeastern Conference Team in 40 years, and for Kentucky, the first time it had played a Big Ten team in 20 years.

A record crowd, 42,311 fans, watched IU defeat Kentucky 12-10 which surpassed the mark of 42,296 set in 1963 against Ohio State. Kentucky jumped out in front early when tailback Roger Gann dashed inside the left end for a 56 touchdown yard run that put the visitors from the Bluegrass State up 7 – 0 . The Wildcats took a 10 – 0 lead when with 1:30 left in the first half, Kentucky place kicker, Dave Weld, connected on a 33 yard field goal after linebacker Gary Shahid recovered a Terry Cole fumble on the Indiana 28.

The Hoosiers came out strong in the second half marching 71 yards in 8 plays during their second series of downs. The drive was capped by a one yard pass from Gonso to Butcher with 3:04 left in the third quarter. In this drive, Gonso ran for 5, then Cole drove across the middle for 5. One play later, Gonso hit Isenbarger on a screen pass at the line of scrimmage. Iso headed west, but quickly reversed his field and ran down the east sidelines for a 42 yard gain. Gonso then spotted split end Eric Stolberg for a nine yard gain, ran around the left end to the one, and then pitched a one yard scoring strike to Butcher who was all alone in the end zone. Warner's kick was wide left and IU trailed 10-6.

Jade Butcher crosses the goal line for the first
of his 30 career TDs and IU's first touchdown of the season.
Indiana University Archives (Kentucky67-1223.8)

After a Kentucky punt, Gonso went to work again. Gonso sprinted out to the left and picked up two huge blocks from Benny Norman and Isenbarger, and raced 63 yards downfield before going out of bounds on the Kentucky 15. Two plays later, Gonso hit tight end Al Gage in the end zone, but the touchdown was nullified due to a penalty for an ineligible receiver down field. Without missing a beat, Gonso dropped back to pass to sophomore Eric

Stolberg, however, Kentucky safety, Bobby Abbott, got his hands on the ball to deflect it. But Cinderella was just starting to try on her shoe, and the deflected pass landed in the outstretched arms of Gage for a 23 yards touchdown pass and IU lead 12-10. The try for the two-point conversion failed and the Hoosiers were left with 14 minutes and 46 seconds to protect a two point lead, which they would do with the help of an outstanding defense.

In the first series, linebacker, Jim Sniadecki, recorded two tackles for lost yardage forcing a punt. Then on the next two series, defensive back, Dave Kornowa, came up with interceptions. Finally, Nate Cunningham intercepted a Kentucky pass with 22 seconds left to seal the victory for the Hoosiers.

Gonso runs for 115 yards in his first varsity game leading the
Hoosiers to a 12-10 victory.
Indiana University Archives (Kentucky67-1235.19)

The sun of that early fall afternoon shown brightest on the sophomore quarterback who carried the ball 25 times for a net gain of 115 yards, while completing 11 of 15 passes for 121 yards, two touchdowns, and no interceptions. His 40 plays ranked him sixth at the time and his 236 yards total offense was at that time seventh best in Indiana history.

The star of that first game, quarterback Harry Gonso, spoke of the Kentucky game saying, "That game quite candidly is a blur. I remember feeling very fortunate to have won that game. It was obviously a great start, each game that followed I can remember more and more clearly. I was not at all nervous as a first game sophomore, I just remember we went out there to execute and try to do things right and limit our mistakes. We ended up winning and we would build on that, it was a season of momentum. We just kept building on success and gaining confidence as we went. This occurred incrementally as the season went along."

Jade Butcher sat across the table with a huge smile on his face as he remembered that game and just simply said that, "Anytime you beat Kentucky, it's special," as he remembered with pride his first college touchdown catch, the one yard pass from Gonso that brought the Hoosiers to within 4 points, 10-6.

Jade's good friend and roommate T-bear, fullback, Terry Cole, spoke to IU's Jon Steine 10 years later about the importance of IU opening victory over Kentucky saying that of all the games that season, the Kentucky stood out more then any other. Cole said, "I went into the opener against Kentucky with more hope and desire for a win than I had ever had in my football career. I sensed this game would set the pace for the season. A victory would reinforce the confidence that was building, ease any doubts, and prime us for the Big Ten. Conversely, a defeat would have shattered morale early. I knew that a defeat in this game would make the season difficult and probably disappointing. I can remember only too well the absolutely sickening feeling that I felt as I watched the Kentucky offense add their tenth unanswered point to the scoreboard. I remember thinking that all the work and effort hadn't gone for naught, and surely this wouldn't happen again. And it didn't. We came back. We held on, and we beat Kentucky, 12-10. The elation that I felt following that game, that most important victory, was due to the pride in what our team had finally become and what I felt certain we could do throughout the season. It was and will always be my most special moment in football."

Terry Cole had expressed it best, for the Hoosiers had started the season with a win of major importance and little did anyone know that for the next seven weekends, the results would mirror that first glorious weekend.

FIRST DOWNS	IU	UK
Total	19	16
Rushing	16	11
Passing	3	5
Penalty	0	0
RUSHING		
Rushes	59	37
Yards Gained	298	215
Yards Lost	40	20
Net Rushing Yardage	258	195
FORWARD PASSING		
Attemped	17	25
Completed	11	11
Intercepted	0	4
Net Yards Passing	121	115
TOTAL PLAYS		
(Rushing and Passes)	76	62
TOTAL NET YARDS	379	310
PUNTING		
Punts	4	3
Average Yards	24	45
Blocked	1*	0
KICK RETURNS		
Punts Returned	3	2
Punt Returned Yardage	29	29
Kickoff Returns	2	3
Kickoff Return Yards	36	57
INTERCEPTION RETURNS		
Returned	4	0
Yards Returned	39	0
FUMBLES		
Fumbles	3	0

Fumbles Lost	2	0
PENALTIES		
Penalties	2	7
Yards Penalized	30	49

*Field goal attempt.

Chapter 3

Indiana vs. Kansas
September 30, 1967
The Battle of the Substitute Kickers

Game two would be against Kansas. It would again take place in Bloomington at Memorial Stadium. This would be the first meeting ever of these two schools on the gridiron. Saturday, Sept. 30, was Band Day where seventy high school bands and over 5,000 band members gave a pre-game show starting a half hour before kickoff.

Indiana would come into the game riding high after their thrilling 12-10 victory over border rival Kentucky. Kansas on the other hand, arrived losers of a heart breaking 21-20 lose to Stanford the previous week at Palo Alto, California. A game in which Kansas lost three fumbles, had three passes intercepted, and in the final two minutes of the game, missed a field goal.

Coach Pont had made two changes to the starting lineup coming into the game, both on defense, as he inserted both Clarence Price and Cal Snowden as starting defensive ends. The Jayhawks would bring speed and size to the Hoosier's second game. The game would mark only the third time in modern history that Kansas would play a Big Ten school. They had beaten Minnesota and lost to Iowa previously, while Indiana had won 13 of 21 games against Big Eight schools, tying 4 other times.

This September day, was a glorious Indian Summer Day and a Band Day crowd of 34,861 showed up; many of them students clutching their one dollar knothole ticket in hand to see if Indiana could start the season 2 and 0 for the first time since 1962, when the Hoosiers had recorded victories over Kansas State and Cincinnati.

Indiana took the opening kick-off and on the second play from scrimmage, sophomore quarterback, Harry Gonso, fumbled the ball when hit by defensive end Vernon Vanoy. Kansas safety, Tommy Ball, recovered the fumble for Kansas on the Indiana

13

two and set up the first score of the game. Kansas quarterback, Bobby Douglass, sneaked across the goal line on the very next play, and following a two point conversion run by flanker Don Shanklin, Kansas was out in front 8-0 with only 89 seconds gone in the opening quarter. Kansas came right back on their second possession to march the ball to the IU 4 yard line only to see the Hoosier defense stiffen and make a brilliant goal line stand. After 3 straight runs by halfback Junior Riggins, who got the ball to the one, a fourth down pass intended for Shanklin in the end zone was knocked away by defensive back Nate Cunningham, thus preserving the 8-0 deficit for the Hoosiers. The score would remain 8-0 in favor of Kansas at the end of the first quarter.

Nate Cunningham #22
and Ken Kaczmarek # 52 make the stop.
Indiana University Archives
(Kansas67-1272.9)

Indiana would finally get on the board in the second quarter with a seven play, sixty-one yard drive. Harry Gonso worked his magic on IU's first scoring drive by passing on the first six plays of the drive. He hit one to Al Gage for 16 yards, one to Ben Norman for 12, and had one pass ruled good for 5 yards on an interference call by Kansas Wippel against Gage. However, the big play of the drive was a 28 yard halfback pass from John Isenbarger to Bloomington's Jade Butcher for IU's first score. Following Indiana's first touchdown, a Gonso to Isenbarger two point conversion pass tied the score at 8-8 with 2:42 left in the first half. The score would remain tied at 8 at halftime.

John Isenbarger #17, not only a threat to run, but to pass as well, launches a strike to Butcher for a 28 yard touchdown.
Indiana University Archives (Kansas67-1270.3)

Indiana would go out in front early in the third period by taking the kick-off and marching downfield 83 yards in eight plays to take the lead. Fullback, Terry Cole, got into the act on this drive with a 16 yard run up the middle followed by a 15 yard face mask penalty. A big third down and eight pass to Mike Krivoshia, and a 34 yard pass to Butcher, which got the ball to the nine yard line, set up the next toss, a nine yard TD pass from Gonso to Butcher. A Kornowa extra point kick made the score 15-8 in favor of IU with 12:58 left in the third quarter. The Jayhawks took advantage of an Isenbarger 22 yard punt that went out of bounds on the IU 41 with 7:36 left in the third to tie the score in 5 plays, capped off by a 19 yard run to the right by Douglass. Bill Bell kicked the extra point and the game would be tied at 15 going into the fourth quarter.

In the fourth quarter, the Hoosier quarterback from Findley, Ohio, took his team 70 yards in 5 plays to set up the eventual winning field goal. A 13 yard pass play to Ben Norman started the drive, then a 39 yard pass to Butcher got the ball to the Kansas 25. Runs by Terry Cole and Mike Krivoshia took the ball to the ten.

Mike Krivoshia on the run against Kansas.
Indiana University Archives (Kansas67-1269.6)

After Krivoshia's four yard run to the six, two incomplete passes brought on senior, Dave Kornowa, kicking for regular kicker, Don Warner, for a 24 yard attempt. The kick was good with 14 minutes and 18 seconds left in the fourth quarter. Indiana led 18-15.

For the second week in a row, the Hoosiers were left with over 14 minutes remaining in the fourth quarter to protect a slim lead. Douglass moved Kansas downfield in the final minutes only to have a pass deflected by Kornowa and picked off by Mike Baughman on the IU twenty. Kansas had one last try as they moved the ball in range for a 27 yard field goal attempt with 32 seconds left. Dave Aikins, who had never before tried a field goal in college, came in to try to tie the score. His attempt was short and wide to the left, and IU had survived another nail biter to win game number two 18-15, allowing IU to win the battle of substitute field goal kickers. Terry Cole would gain 61 yards on the day and John Isenbarger would add 59 for the Hoosiers.

Isenbarger #11 running behind Don Ghrist #52.
Indiana University Archives (Kansas67-1273.11)

Elsewhere around the Big Ten, Purdue would beat Notre Dame 28-21, Nebraska would be victorious over Minnesota 7-0, and no one would be aware that these three Big Ten schools would be destined to finish in a dog fight with each other for the Big Ten Title and a Rose Bowl bid.

FIRST DOWNS	IU	KU
Total	21	15
Rushing	10	9
Passing	8	5
Penalty	3	1
RUSHING		
Rushes	48	49
Yards Gained	172	181

Yards Lost	59	35
Net Rushing Yardage	113	146
FORWARD PASSING		
Attemped	24	22
Completed	11	6
Intercepted	0	1
Net Yards Passing	183	123
TOTAL PLAYS		
(Rushing and Passes)	72	71
TOTAL NET YARDS	296	269
PUNTING		
Punts	9	8
Average Yards	36	40
Blocked	0	0
KICK RETURNS		
Punts Returned	6	5
Punt Returned Yardage	27	57
Kickoff Returns	3	3
Kickoff Return Yards	49	65
INTERCEPTION RETURNS		
Returned	1	0
Yards Returned	8	1
FUMBLES		
Fumbles	2	0
Fumbles Lost	1	0
PENALTIES		
Penalties	5	8
Yards Penalized	31	71

Chapter 4

Indiana vs. Illinois
October 7, 1967

The Defense Stars

Game three featured Indiana's first road contest. The Hoosiers went to Champaign hoping to become the first Indiana football team to open the season 3 and 0 since the 1928 football season. Illinois would come into the game as a 12 point favorite over the Hoosiers, and a crowd of over 53,000 was expected on this I-Mens' Day (this I would be for Illinois) at Zuppke Field.

The biggest irony of the day was the fact that the Illinois football team would be playing their first Big Ten football game since the sanctions and punishment imposed by both the Big Ten and the NCAA the past winter for the famous slush-

Quarterback Harry Gonso
Indiana University Archives (966-0248.9)

fund scandal. The irony would be that Illinois was facing an IU program that had also been the recipient of NCAA punishments and sanctions from 1961-65 because of recruiting violations in football. The sanctions Indiana incurred cost the Indiana Men's swimming and diving team an NCAA Championship, and certainly hurt the men's basketball programs ability to recruit, while neither of these teams had committed any violations and the penalties were the result of the football team improprieties. Unknown to most during this time period, Coach Phil Dickens, a true southern gentleman, would produce what he felt was evidence that Indiana's recruiting was no different than many other schools in the Big Ten. However, President Herman Wells would explain to Coach Dickens, he was only concerned with IU's compliance with the rules, and the standards set at Indiana would be as high as possible. Indiana would observe the NCAA sanctions. Both Indiana and the Big Ten appealed the severity of the penalties on the other sports to no avail.

Indiana faced an Illinois team that came into the game with a 1 and 1 record, losing its' opener to Florida 14-0, only to recover with a 34-6 victory over Pittsburg led by Rich Johnson's 116 rushing yards in only 17 tries. Illinois led the series with Indiana 20 to 7 with 2 ties.

Coach Pont would make two changes for this game, one being that Brown Marks, a former starter from a year ago, would replace injured Bob Moynihan at outside linebacker as Moynihan had suffered a broken leg in practice on Wednesday. Marks had been sidelined all fall with an injury of his own. The second move would be to start Kevin Duffy at inside linebacker. Duffy was coming back from a horrendous injury in the Michigan State game the previous season.

Ken Kaczmarek recalled that, "It was a cloudy, misty day during the pre-game warm-ups; just a crummy day. The team returned to the locker room and everyone was just sitting around thinking about the game. All of a sudden, the sun came through the locker room windows, and you could see it sliding across the locker room floor and either Cal Snowdon or Bob Russell started whistling, He's Got the Whole World in His Hands, and you could just feel the pickup before the game." Kaczmarek said, "I asked Coach Pont if he would let the seniors talk before the game and he said fine. We just talked about that we had an opportunity here, and you could just see it."

Illinois' Carson Brooks, fumbled on the second Illinois play after the kick-off, and Indiana's Price recovered on the Illinois 27 to set up Indiana's first score. Indiana, now on offense, saw Gonso hit Benny Norman for a 20 yard gain to the seven, and then

Isenbarger took the hand-off and was headed for the end zone, when he coughed up the ball at the two. The ball bounced into the end zone where tackle, Rick Spickard, alertly recovered for IU's first score. A Kornow kick made the score 7-0 with just 85 seconds gone in the game. Afterward, a grateful Isenbarger congratulated Spickard on the recovery, joking with him that tackles don't often get to score a touchdown. Indiana's touchdown would be the only score of the first quarter.

Illinois would use 3 different quarterbacks on the day, as starter Bob Naponic was knocked out by a jarring tackle administered by sophomore Karl Pankratz from Toledo, Ohio on the second play of the second quarter. Second string quarterback Bob Bess came in and soon after, left the game with a head injury that would prove not to be serious. Third string quarterback Dean Volkman, a former Evansville North star, entered the contest as Illinois' third quarterback of the day and ended up finishing the game for the Illini.

The only score of the second quarter would also belong to the Hoosiers, as they began a late second quarter drive which began with a Mike Krivoshia fumble that went for a 5 yard gain when guard Gary Cassells recovered for Indiana. Illinois was then assessed a penalty that set the ball down on the Illinois 34 yard line. Tailback John Isenbarger ran for 8 yards before Gonso rolled out for a 13 yard run moving the ball to the Illinois 12. Gonso again rolled out on the next snap, and gained 9 more yards down to the Illinois 3. Two plays later Gonso threw to a wide open Jade Butcher, and Indiana had its second touchdown of the day. A Don Warner kick would be wide right, and the score would remain 13 to 0 in favor of Indiana.

The third quarter was a scoreless affair with neither team being able to do much offensively. In the fourth quarter, with Indiana facing a third and 5 in their own territory, John Isenbarger got off a booming 63 yard punt only to have the kick called back because of an illegal motion penalty. The Hoosiers again went with the quick kick that Illinois was ready for this time. The Illini blocked the kick back into the end zone. Larry Jordan fell on the ball for Illinois' first score. Following a McKissic kick, Indiana lead Illinois 13 to 7 with 12:58 to go in the contest.

21

This game would be typical of the Hoosier's season, a game not decided until the very last minute. With Indiana leading 13 to 7 with less then 4:30 to go in the contest, outside linebacker Brown Marks in his first start of the season, hit Illinois quarterback Dean Volkman, as he was attempting to pitch the ball to tailback Rich Johnson, jarring the ball loose. Senior Jim Sniadecki recovered the fumble on the Indiana 30, and the Hoosiers would take possession of the ball. Unable to move the ball, the Hoosiers punted the ball back to the Illini.

The Illini would have one last chance to erase the 13-7 deficit and capture their second victory of the young season. Indiana, on the other hand, was trying to capture their third win in as many tries. What occurred next was becoming a very familiar pattern to the Hoosier faithful, yet another big defensive stop as senior linebacker Ken Kaczmarek would step in and intercept Volkman's pass and race 28 yards to score a touchdown for the Hoosiers with 2:01 left in the contest. "We knew they were going to throw hooks and things like that." Kaczmarek recalled, "We just dropped back into our hook zone, and I just moved to where I thought the quarterback was going to throw the ball. After the touchdown, I threw the ball into the stands and all of a sudden Coach Pont came up and jumped on me. Then everyone joined him, so we had kind of a big pile up there and that was a very emotional time."

During the game, Big Ten Weightlifting Champion, Fritz Barns, had been giving the Hoosier offensive line fits trying to contain his rush. Center Mauro recalled, "Harry, always the talker, would come up to the line and yell across the line to Fritz, 'Hey Fritz let's see if you can catch me on this play.' Finally back in the huddle the linemen said, 'Harry just shut up! We're having a hard enough time blocking them as it is, if you don't shut up were just going to fall down and let them come in and kill you.' "

With the win, the Hoosiers had won their first game in Champaign since 1945. The symbolism would become more significant as the season wore on and the Hoosiers would go on to their first Big Ten Title since that '45 campaign. Two events of the day highlighted the significance of the win. Bob Russell came up to Gonso on the bus ride home, sitting next to him and saying, "You know Harry, I think we are for real." The team stopped for a prime rib dinner, and even Pont said he was going to eat two himself because he was so happy with the outcome of the game. Arriving in Bloomington, the team was surprised to see fans in the parking lot passing out roses. After game three, the seed was firmly planted. Or was it a rose bush?

FIRST DOWNS	IU	IL
Total	12	22
Rushing	7	14
Passing	4	6
Penalty	1	2
RUSHING		
Rushes	38	49
Yards Gained	157	175
Yards Lost	29	38
Net Rushing Yardage	128	137
FORWARD PASSING		
Attemped	14	28
Completed	9	14
Intercepted	0	1
Net Yards Passing	61	125
TOTAL PLAYS		
(Rushing and Passes)	52	77
TOTAL NET YARDS	189	262
PUNTING		
Punts	8	4
Average Yards	34.1	41.3
Blocked	1	0
KICK RETURNS		
Punts Returned	2	4
Punt Returned Yardage	10	13

Kickoff Returns	2	3
Kickoff Return Yards	41	34
INTERCEPTION RETURNS		
Returned	1	0
Returned Yards	26	0
FUMBLES		
Fumbles	4	5
Fumbles Lost	0	2
PENALTIES		
Penalties	8	4
Yards Penalized	78	34

Chapter 5

Indiana vs. Iowa
October 14, 1967
Gambling Harry

It was Saturday, October 14, a Dads' Day crowd of over 41,000 would come to see if these Cardiac Kids of John Pont could start the Indiana football season with four straight wins for the first time since 1910. The official game day program appropriately enough featured a golden football set amongst gold leaves in the midst of what would become a truly golden season. The students on Friday night could go to the Indiana Theatre and watch The Family Way starring John & Haley Mills, with music by the Beatle's Paul McCartney, or go to the Princess and see The Best Picture of the Year, A Man for All Seasons, starring Best Actor, Paul Scofield.

Coming into the game, quarterback Harry Gonso, and flanker Jade Butcher, who along with their teammates were becoming a football team for all seasons, had combined for a touchdown in every collegiate game they had played in for Indiana University; consisting of 2 freshman games in 1966 and all 3 games of the '67 season to that point in time. To underscore the kind of offensive line blocking the Hoosiers were getting, fullback Terry Cole, and halfback Mike Krivoshia, had yet to lose a yard rushing that fall in 57 attempts. Cole, a senior from Mitchell, had gained 168 yards in 38 tries, and Krivoshia, a senior from Midland, PA., had accounted for 74 yards in 19 carries.

Iowa came into the game with a record of 1-2 winning their first game over Texas Christian 24-9, before losing to both Oregon State and Notre Dame. Iowa had defeated the '66 IU team 20-19 at Iowa City. IU came into the game ranked 18th, their first national ranking since 1945. IU's sophomore sensation, quarterback Harry Gonso, was held out of practice Thursday because of a viral infection, which had the Indiana faithful holding their collective breath.

It was a beautiful autumn day that Saturday, and as the 1:30 kick-off rolled around, the crowd was just settling in their seats with the exception of the knothole section on the west side of the stadium. Anxious youngsters were leaping, jumping, and even diving onto the metal bleachers, hoping to catch one of the white plastic mini footballs thrown into the stands, compliments of Colonial Bread, and featuring a picture of Memorial Stadium on it. The mini footballs would not be the only thing thrown that day,

26

as with 1:04 left in the game, the Hoosiers would throw caution to the wind in an effort to secure yet another victory.

Butcher #40 and Nate Cunningham #22 on run back.
Indiana University Archives (Iowa67-1303.15)

The scoring for the game started as Gonso rolled to his left and was met by three Iowa defenders. Harry fumbled the ball, which was recovered by Hawkeye Steve Wilson on the Indiana 29. Iowa ran the next play up the middle for 10 yards. The strong Hoosier defense stiffened, and Iowa was unable to move the football, forcing the Hawkeye's to settle for an Anderson 30 yard field goal, which gave Iowa an early 3-0 lead with 9:07 left in the first quarter. Indiana would then come back to score on their next possession of the first quarter on a nine play 73 yard drive that featured a 47 yard run on a Gonso keeper. He started to sprint out to his left and received key blocks by both Cole and Isenbarger. Gonso cut back right racing down and across the field until tackled at the Iowa 21. Terry Cole took the next snap up the middle, followed by John Isenbarger going off right tackle, then another Cole plunge up the middle. Gonso would then sprint around the left side of the line to the 10. A holding penalty gave IU the ball first and goal at the one. On the next play, a hand-off to Isenbarger resulted in a two yard loss back to the three. Gonso then rolled out to his right, and finding Butcher near the right end of the end zone, lofted a perfect pass over the defender that nestled in Jade's arms for six points. Indiana led 7-3 following the extra point kick, with 5:23 to go in the first quarter. Gonso and Butcher had now combined for a 4th straight game to play pitch and catch for a Hoosier touchdown.

Crusan #78 and Price #96 stop Hawkeyes.
Indiana University Archives (Iowa67-1303.2)

In the second quarter, one of the themes of the season took place for IU, as John Isenbarger, back on his own 5, pulled down the punt attempt and ran the ball to the Hoosier 35 for a first down. John explained the coaches had noticed during the film session of that week, that when Iowa was in a six man line, "They would hit and just turn their backs, and I would run right behind them." Later in the quarter, after an Isenbarger punt pinned Iowa down at their own 4 yard line, a great Hoosier defensive stance forced an Iowa kick that was tipped and went out of bounds on the Hawkeye 33. The Hoosiers would take advantage of the wonderful field position as back-up quarterback Mike Perry, subbing for Gonso who was still feeling the effects of a viral infection, moved the ball to the Hawkeye 9 with the help of a pass interference call on a pass intended for Eric Stolberg. Gonso would return to finish the drive by hitting Butcher with a pass, sprinting out to his right down the sideline to the 3. Cole ran up the middle to the 1, which set up the last play of the drive, as Gonso handed the ball off to Mike Krivoshia for a one yard plunge. Following Warner's extra point, the Hoosiers led 14 to 3 with 1:49 to go in the second quarter.

The Hawkeyes took the second half kick-off and drove 61 yards with quarterback Ed Podolak passing to Paul Usinowicg for an 11 yard strike to make the score 14-10. After the Iowa touchdown, IU threatened to get another one of its own as Gonso passed 39 yards to Butcher on the Iowa 28. The drive stalled on the Iowa 25, and Indiana elected to try a Warner 42 yard field goal. The attempt was short and the third quarter came to a close with the Hoosiers still in command 14-10.

With McKinnie running and Podolak throwing in the fourth, Iowa marched down the field for what looked like might be the last score of the game. The drive ended with a one yard sneak by Podolak, and the kick by Anderson gave the Hawkeyes a 3 point lead with 3:48 to go in the game.

The stage was now set, and Indiana was about to play out the final act, as John Isenbarger took Jim Crousis' kick-off at the 7 and raced up field to the Hoosier 40 for a 33 yard gain. Gonso then rolled to his right, getting hit 3 times before going down at the 50, gaining just enough for a first down. Gonso then rolled to his left and gained 9 yards to the 41. Substitute fullback , Roger Grove, from Port Wentworth, Georgia, carried the ball to the 31 for a first down. Gonso hit end Al Gage at the 20. Isenbarger could gain nothing on the next play, then a Gonso pass that was over Ben Norman's head at the 5 left it third and ten. Gonso went back to pass and eluded a fierce rush by Iowa's John Hendricks, but was still tackled for a 2 yard loss, setting up a fourth and 12 on the Iowa 22. Indiana called a time out, and Gonso later recalled discussing the fake field goal. The Hoosiers knew that Iowa would probably be looking for a fake, so in this chess match, called a Big Ten football game, the Hoosiers believed that an I thought, you thought mentality, might result in Iowa actually believing a field goal attempt would be made. The decision was made to go with the fake, and the Hoosiers returned to the field.

Don Warner # 42 makes a stop.
Indiana University Archives (Iowa67-1305.4)

The moans began to go up in the student section for what they perceived was a field goal attempt to tie the game. While in the alumni section, many heads nodded their approval, for to them, a tie was better than a loss, and with a minute remaining, those seemed to be the only options. However, Gonso knew better. Gonso leaped to take the snap on a run or pass option, with the play evolving in what seemed like slow motion. Under the fixed eyes of the Hoosier faithful, Harry dashed around the left end to the Iowa 4. Eyes wide open and mouths agape, the Hoosier fans began to breathe again as the Hoosiers were still alive with a first and goal on the Iowa 4. IU called another time out with 58 seconds left to set up the winning play. IU came to the line, and Gonso took the snap from Mauro, rolling out and waiting for Jade to free himself from his defenders. At the last second, Gonso released the ball as Butcher leaped high between two defenders and secured his sixth touchdown pass of the season, his second of the game, and the winning catch on this afternoon. Later, Butcher would explain, "Harry was just too much; you could see it in his eyes. I looked at the clock and said, gee, we've got to do something quick, so Harry rolls out and I am running the side lines, then he gets in trouble, he goes back to the middle, and I go back to the middle, and I catch it. That was something special, really special. That

30

is why Harry and I would stay after practice working on routes and getting to know each others' routes, to enable us to complete passes like the one against Iowa."

Iowa would take the final kick-off back to the nine and would actually have time to get off seven plays. The backbone of this Hoosier team, the veteran defense, were at their swarming best. The defense featuring seniors, Duffy, Kaczmarek, Crusan, Sniadecki, Gill, Kornowa, and Marks along with juniors, Baughman, Grecco, Snowden, and Bilunas, would not allow

Butcher holds the ball high, as was his tradition, after scoring the winning TD over Iowa. Courtesy: Jade Butcher

Podolak time to get off a good pass, and IU would hold on for a 21-17 win. Afterward, Pont explained that Isenbarger's first fake punt was planned, but on the second attempt, Iowa had seven instead of six men on the line and that a punt was indeed called for on this occasion. Isenbarger later recalled that it was the '60's and we were what they called "free thinkers," "I just pretty much react in sports."

This Indiana team was coming together and was giving the college football world evidence of why they would earn the nickname the Cardiac Kids. The offense was the daring, dashing, and swashbuckling unit that did not know their own limits, and the defense would be what the late Terry Hoeppner would call Memorial Stadium years later, The Rock, upon which Pont would build his championship team. Indiana was now 4 and 0 with the win over Iowa, and the following week the UPI would rank the Hoosiers fourteenth; and the special season would continue.

FIRST DOWNS	IU	IA
Total	15	18
Rushing	10	13
Passing	4	4
Penalty	1	1
RUSHING		
Yards Gained	239	253
Yards Lost	36	45
Net Rushing Yardage	203	208
FORWARD PASSING		
Attemped	19	14
Completed	7	4
Intercepted	1	1
Net Yards Passing	114	62
TOTAL PLAYS		
(Rushing and Passes)	75	69
TOTAL NET YARDS	317	270
PUNTING		
Punts	6	8
Average Yards	42	42
Blocked	0	0
KICK RETURNS		
Punts Returned	4	3
Punt Returned Yardage	12	27
Kickoff Returns	5	4
Kickoff Return Yards	92	82
INTERCEPTION RETURNS		
Returns	1	1
Return Yards	33	5
FUMBLES		
Fumbles	3	1

Fumbles Lost	1	1
PENALTIES		
Penalties	4	7
Yards Penalized	41	55

Chapter 6

Indiana vs. Michigan
October 21, 1967
Punt John, Punt

Captain Doug Crusan
Indiana University Archives (966-0248.9)

The fifth weekend of the season brought game five against the traditional powerhouse, Michigan Wolverines. The game would be played in Ann Arbor, and back in Bloomington, the radios were tuned to WTTS at 12:30 local time to see if the Hoosiers could start the season 5 and 0, for the first time in Indiana's 82 year history. Could Indiana take its' Big Ten record to 3-0 and continue to share the conference lead? Some die hard fans even dared to whisper whether IU could keep the dream of a January 1st date in Pasadena alive. Michigan was a shadow of the '66 team that had fought for the conference title, loosing fourteen regulars, eight of which had been drafted by the AFL or NFL. The Wolverines were 1-3, but still featured powerful runningback Ron Johnson, who had gained 512 yards in 89 attempts.

Sixty-five thousand, seven hundred, twenty-nine watched in horror as Indiana scored on their first two possessions on that sunny October day. Indiana started their first drive on the 23 and moved the ball 77 yards for their first score of the game. One of the two big plays of that drive came when Isenbarger lofted a pass to an all alone Jade Butcher, for 38 yards. Isenbarger then rambled 26 yards, breaking tackles along the way, scoring the Hoosier's first touchdown. A Warner kick made it 7-0, and the outlook for the Hoosiers seemed rosy.

On their next possession, Michigan's Johnson fumbled the ball, and senior Doug Crusan of Indiana recovered on the Wolverine's 33 yard line. The Hoosiers would take only 5 plays to score again. The drive started with an 8 yard run by fullback Terry Cole, followed by runs of 13 and 4 yards by Mike Krivoshia. The ball was on the 8, and Gonso set up in the pocket and drilled an aerial spiral to sophomore, Eric Stolberg. Don Warner's second extra point attempt made the score Indiana 14, Michigan 0, with only 9:13 played in the first quarter.

In the second quarter, another Michigan fumble, one of eight fumbles lost during the day, four by each team, gave the Hoosiers the ball back on the Michigan 41. Quickly, Indiana using the half back option pass for the second time in the game, connected on a 41 yard scoring strike from Isenbarger to Butcher. The extra point kick failed, and Indiana led 20-0 with 7:22 to go in the first half. Michigan responded with a scoring drive of their own going 47 yards in 9 plays. The final play of that drive was a 3 yard run by quarterback Dennis Brown. The extra point try was successful, and the scoreboard read Indiana 20, Michigan 7, at the end of the first half.

The third quarter saw sophomore John Isenbarger's, third pass of the afternoon intercepted by Michigan safety, Tom Curtis, on the Michigan 45. The Hoosier turnover set up the Wolverine's second touchdown. Brown, starting his first game at quarterback for the Wolverines, moved Michigan 55 yards in 8 plays for Michigan's second score of the game. Brown would carry the ball over the goal line himself making the score 20-14, and Indiana went into the fourth quarter with a slim 6 point lead, just like the previous week with Iowa. And just like the previous week, things would become more than a bit strange. Indiana took over on downs on its own 5, after holding the Michigan offense out of the end zone. Indiana, unable to move the ball the required 10 yards for a first down, was forced to punt on a fourth and two with the ball resting on the Indiana 13.

Isenbarger went back to punt just as he did the previous Saturday against Iowa, and just like the week before, Isenbarger pulled down the ball and began to run for a first down. Again like the week before, he failed, this time because he was hit and fumbled the ball on the Indiana 16. As John said, "We were free thinkers, no one knew except for myself that I was going to run the fake punt. After I fumbled the ball, and Michigan took over, I came to our sidelines and a fuming coach Pont told me to sit on the bench. To this day, it could have been the last play I ever played for IU." Michigan, taking advantage of the golden opportunity, saw quarterback Dennis Brown run for 12 yards. At the end of the run, a flag was thrown as a personal foul was assessed against the Hoosiers. The personal foul would take the ball to the one. Halfback Johnson then carried the ball the last yard into the end zone, and the one time lead of 20-0 had evaporated to a 20-20 tie.

The play by Isenbarger would lead to the following week's chant of Punt John, Punt. The previous week's indiscretion had lead to a 17-13 Hawkeye lead, now the score was tied at 20, but the strangeness of the game was not over. After Indiana took the kick off, Mike Krivoshia fumbled on the very next play, and Michigan's Gerald Hartman recovered on the Indiana 28. On a fourth and four play, Brown completed a 9 yard pass to halfback John Gabler for a first down on the Indiana 13. Michigan combined on the next two plays for 8 yards, but on a third and two, Indiana stopped Johnson for no gain, and sophomore Mike Hankwitz came in to attempt the field goal. The kick was low and off to the left, and with 4:40 remaining in the game, Indiana took over on its own 20.

Isenbarger was still sitting, and Pont was still fuming, as the

Indiana offense prepared to come back onto the field. Gonso approached Pont with the plea that the team needed Isenbarger on the field. Pont later recalled that, "I thought John was safer on the field with Harry than sitting on the bench next to me."

The Hoosiers would then march 11 plays and 80 yards for the winning score. Isenbarger ran around the right end for 8 yards, and Butcher caught a pass from Gonso for a first down on the 35. After a 1 yard run by Isenbarger, Gonso hit Gage for a 31 yard pass completion to the Michigan 22. Isenbarger picked up another first down with a 10 yard run and carried again for 6, down to the 17. Cole plunged over the middle for 4 to the 13, and Indiana had another first down. Iso ran around the right end for 8 and then the left end for 4. Cole ran for 1, then Isenbarger, finishing what he had started, and shedding his goat horns for a hero's laurel, ran across the goal line with 1:14 left, and Indiana led 26-20. Warner's kick made it Indiana 27, Michigan 20, and all that was left was for IU to hold onto the lead.

Brown was moving Michigan one last time, when Dave Kornowa intercepted Brown's pass at the Indiana 23 with 15 seconds to play. Indiana's defense had come up with yet another big turnover to preserve yet another huge win.

On the day, Doug Crusan, Brown Marks, Ken Kaczmarek, Jim Sniadecki, Kevin Duffy, and Nate Cunningham had led the defense. Crusan recovered 2 fumbles, made 6 solo tackles, and had 4 assists, while Marks had 11 solo tackles and 3 assists. Kaczmarek would match Marks total with 7 solo tackles and 7 assists. Cunningham would have 8 tackles, while Sniadecki added 7.

During the week, before the game, Doug Crusan had asked coach Pont if he could switch back to the offensive line, because he just didn't feel he was contributing enough on defense. Crusan told Pont that he just didn't think he was getting enough tackles to help the team. Pont explained that his job was also to occupy two people at the same time, and allow the other defensive players to go after the ball, and that he was doing a great job. After the Michigan game, the Midwest Lineman of the week, Captain Doug Crusan, thought that this defensive thing might just be working out alright.

FIRST DOWNS	IU	UM
Total	18	22
By Rushing	13	10
By Passing	5	12
By Penalty	0	0
RUSHING		
No. of Rushes	52	56
Yards Gained	239	202
Yards Lost	21	14
Net Rushing Yardage	218	188
FORWARD PASSING		
Number Attemped	14	31
Number Completed	7	18
No. Had Intercepted	1	1
Net Yards Passing	157	211
TOTAL PLAYS		
(Rushing and Passes)	66	87
TOTAL NET YARDS	375	399
PUNTING		
Number of Punts	4	2
Average Yards	36.7	55
Had Blocked	0	0
KICK RETURNS		
No. of Punts Returned	1	2
Punt Returned Yardage	9	11
No. of Kickoff Returns	4	4
Kickoff Return Yards	56	103
INTERCEPTION RETURNS		
Number Returned	1	1
Yards Returned	4	0

FUMBLES

No. of Fumbles	4	4
Fumbles Lost	4	4

PENALTIES

No. of Penalties	8	3
Yards Penalized	45	25

Chapter 7

Indiana vs. Arizona
October 28, 1967
Jade's Night to Shine

Indiana entered week six of their golden season in very unfamiliar territory. They joined such football powers as Southern California, UCLA, Virginia Tech, and Colorado as unbeaten major universities for the '67 football season. There were only eleven universities in all standing undefeated with North Carolina State, Wyoming, East Carolina, Dartmouth, Harvard, and Tulsa rounding out the group.

Courtesy: Jade Butcher

The Hoosiers would meet Arizona at 9:00 p.m. on Saturday, October 28, Bloomington time. Arizona came into the game with a 1-3-1 record, however, they had defeated the Ohio State Buckeyes 14-7, and one loss was to eighth ranked Wyoming. Arizona employed a 4-3-4 defense that featured a huge front line that outweighed Indiana's offensive line by an average of 24 lbs.

Going into the game, quarterback Harry Gonso led the Hoosiers in total offense with 778 yards on 249 rushing yards in 87 carries, as well as 529 passing yards on 42 out of 80 passes. Halfback John Isenbarger led IU in rushing, with 271 yards that averaged out to 4.5 yards per carry, coming off his best game at Michigan in which he rushed for 101 yards on 18 carries. Jade Butcher had already caught 20 passes for 322 yards and 7 touchdowns. Doug Crusan led the defense that had recorded 57 tackles and 5 turnovers against Michigan, earning him Midwest Lineman of the week honors.

This game marked the first time the two schools, representing the Big Ten and the Western Athletic Conference, had ever played each other on the gridiron. Students and alumni tuned into the broadcast over WTTS, or WTTV-FM, the IU sports network, to see if the upstart Hoosiers could win a sixth in a row.

The Hoosiers arrived in Arizona greeted by a press, that in editorial sports' cartoons, depicted the Hoosiers as a farmer sitting on a tractor with straw stuck out of his mouth, a total hay seed. The team later expressed that they were really ticked off, and it was a motivating factor as the Hoosiers approached the game.

Meanwhile, before the game, two teammates would joke with one another. Butcher later recalled Terry Cole saying to him, "Hey, Jade, this might be your thing. You know, it's a night game, you love night games, you play great in night games. He was right; to me night games are great. I was in a zone that night, but remember, the quarterbacks, Harry and Mike Perry, were in the zone as well. They were the ones making the passes. I had 3 touchdowns, but my 61 yard punt return was called back by a clip." A knothole kid himself, he said it was really special to break Bill Malinchak's record during the Arizona game, remembering that both Malinchak and John Ginter were his idols in high school. "The thing that made this team, the game, and the season so good was that we played the way we practiced, and we practiced hard."

Indiana came out in their first drive and needed only four plays to score. Gonso, pitching to Isenbarger, saw his halfback rumble 9 yards to the Arizona 47. Cole had a quick hitter to the 44, and then Gonso connected with Jade Butcher at the Arizona 15, and Jade carried Arizona cornerback Willy Scott all the way down to the sixth. What followed would be great blocking on the left side of the offensive line by Spickard, Cassells, and Mauro to allow Isenbarger to score IU's first touchdown, and after Warner's kick, IU lead 7-0 with the game but 3 minutes old.

On IU's second possession, Gonso sprinted 49 yards down field to the Arizona one. He actually made it into the end zone;

however, the official ruled he had stepped out at the one. This set up the second touchdown, which would prove to be both difficult and costly to the Hoosiers. On the next play, Gonso carried the ball into the end zone again on a quarterback sneak, only to have the touchdown nullified by a penalty that took the ball back to the six. Isenbarger took the next possession and ran the ball back to the one. Gonso again tried the quarterback sneak into the end zone, and this time, the play stood and IU led 13-0. However, in the process, Gonso suffered a bruised shoulder and left the game after only six minutes of action with the Hoosiers leading 13-0.

Junior Mike Perry from Indianapolis, the back-up for Gonso, who had played in only two games the previous year and appeared only briefly in the Iowa game this season, came in for the injured Gonso to direct the team for the last 54 minutes of the game. Perry's inspirational play led the Hoosiers to 29 more points in the last 3 quarters, passing for 157 yards including one touchdown pass, a 73 yard bomb to Jade Butcher, and running the football for an additional 40 yards. He also ran in 2 two-point conversions. IU went up 19-0 on Butcher's eighth touchdown catch of the season, a 12 yard strike from halfback Isenbarger. That catch broke Bill Malinchak's school season record of seven.

In the final minutes of the first half, Arizona blocked a punt and recovered it on the Indiana 22, then connected on a 20 yard pass from Higuera to Reed to make the score 19-7 at the end of the first 30 minutes.

Arizona early in the third quarter, intercepted an Indiana pass and drove the ball all the way to the Indiana 20, before being stopped by IU's defense on the Indiana 17. Taking over, the Hoosiers drove swiftly down the field led by Perry's 40 yard run. Isenbarger added a big gain as he went around the right end on a 37 yard run that put the ball on the Arizona six. On a fourth and one, fullback Terry Cole crossed the end zone, and following a Perry run for a two point conversion, the Hoosiers lead 27-7.

Arizona, forced to try to get back into the game, came out firing, and a Nate Cunningham 55 yard interception return, with another Perry two point conversion run, had the guests from Bloomington in the unfamiliar position of being up 35-7 going into the fourth quarter.

The only scoring to take place in the final quarter would be the 73 yard strike from Perry to Butcher giving the Bloomington native 5 catches, 175 yards, and two touchdowns on the day, in a most dominating performance. When the final gun went off, the Hoosiers had delighted the fans, both the ones at the game and the ones listening at home, with a 42-7 victory over the host Arizona Wildcats.

FIRST DOWNS	IU	AZ
Total	14	13
RUSHING		
Net Rushing Yardage	228	66
FORWARD PASSING		
Attemped	11	33
Completed	7	15
Intercepted	1	2
Net Yards Passing	207	181
PUNTING		
Punts	6	8
Average Yards	44.3	45
FUMBLES		
Fumbles	1	4
Fumbles Lost	0	0
PENALTIES		
Penalties	9	4
Yards Penalized	74	29

Chapter 8

Indiana vs. Wisconsin
November 4, 1967
Homecoming

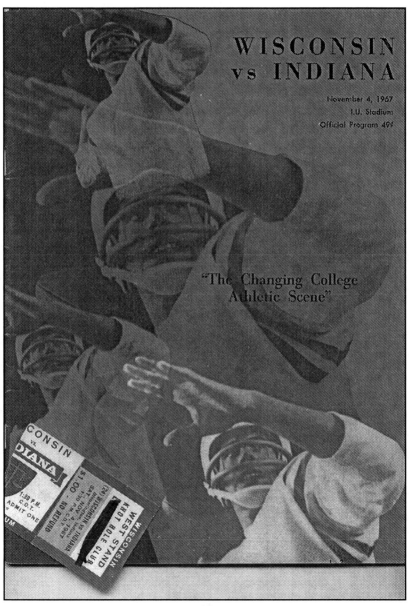

Saturday, November 4, was Homecoming in Bloomington, Indiana. The 1:30 p.m. game featured the Cinderella Hoosiers at 6 and 0 against the winless Wisconsin Badgers at 0-5-1. Students gathered at Nicks, decorated the dorms, sororities and fraternities, as well as floats, in anticipation of the undefeated Hoosiers adding win number seven to their record. The movie at the Indiana starring Lee Marvin and Angie Dickinson, Point Blank, seemed to echo the sentiments of everyone that the Hoosiers were point blank favorites to win contest number 7 and stay atop the Big Ten standings.

The 42 points scored the week before, were the most by an IU football team since a 48-14 victory over Pittsburg in 1949. Jade Butcher had become the second straight Hoosier named UPI Midwest Lineman of the week following senior defensive tackle Doug Crusan, who won the honor for his performance in the Michigan game the week before. Butcher's remarkable day in the land of the sun had earned him those honors.

Gonso on the run lead by Rick Spickard # 79 and Bob Russell # 64.
Indiana University Archives (Wisconsin67-1394.8)

This was the first time IU played Wisconsin since 1962, with Indiana's last victory coming in 1948. Indiana's offensive line play had continued to sparkle as senior guard Bob Russell, tightend Al Gage, tackle Rick Spickard, guard Gary Cassells, center Harold Mauro, and tackle Bob Kirk were all graded at making over 70% of their blocks, Russell and Gage at almost 80% (79%). The secondary had already intercepted 10 passes on the season, one more than all of last year, led by cornerbacks Dave Kornowa and Nate Cunningham who had each picked off three.

The Big Wheel Restaurant on College was packed that morning with an early game day crowd anticipating a Homecoming to remember. Families stopped at the Roto-Lite Drive Inn at 11th and Walnut to grab hamburgers and fries, sliding down their silver bins as quickly as Gonso and Isenbarger had hit open holes in the line all season, or the defense had tackled would-be runners.

The City Council of Bloomington by unanimous consent, passed a resolution to be sent to IU football coach, John Pont and the team wishing them the best of luck in Saturday's Homecoming game against the University of Wisconsin. Councilman Richard Fee had written the resolution, and as one councilman pointed out, their letter on October 19, before the Michigan game did so much good, just think what a resolution will do!

Gonso sweeps on a keeper as Fred Mitchell #91 looks for a block.
Indiana University Archives (Wisconsin67-1388.5)

Hoosier faithful were assured sophomore sensation, Harry Gonso, shaken up in the 42-7 victory over Arizona, was fit, healthy, and ready to play. Knothole fans noticed that a black mark covered up their seating area, as 2,000 temporary bleacher seats were to be added to the end zones to move stadium capacity beyond it's normal 48,344 to over 50,000 with a homecoming crowd beginning to believe that maybe, just maybe, there were indeed roses in IU's future. Unlike the other three Saturday home games, this one was cold and cloudy with occasional light snow flurries whipping through the stadium, as if all 46,910 spectators, stadium and all, were encased in a giant snow globe that the football gods had just shaken up.

Indiana scored in the first quarter as Jade Butcher was hit attempting to make a fair catch on a punt to move the ball to Wisconsin's 31. Six plays later, a Gonso to Isenbarger 15 yard pass play, and a Warner extra point kick, put Indiana ahead 7-0 with 8:14 left in the first quarter.

In the second quarter, Wisconsin moved early to within field goal range, and Tom Schinke kicked a 27 yard field goal with 14:22 left in the second quarter to make the score a close 7-3. The score remained, as neither team was able to muster much of a drive the rest of the first half. As both teams struggled to get their offense going, there were 13 total punts on the day to go along with 5 turnovers.

Defense surrounds Bilunas # 80; Marks #84, Kornowa #14, Crusan #78, Snowden #61, and Kaczmarek #52.
Indiana University Archives (Wisconsin67-1393.2)

Indiana's big break came late in the third quarter when Brown Marks intercepted a Boyajian pass on the Wisconsin 27, and IU looked as if they could get their second score of the day. On the Indiana drive, Gonso fumbled the ball, and Wisconsin's Lynn Bass recovered for the Badgers. However, a holding penalty against Wisconsin gave the ball back to the Hoosiers with a first down on the Wisconsin 3. Mike Krivoshia went over the left guard for one, and then Mike Perry got stopped just short of the goal line. Krivoshia then carried the pigskin in for the touchdown, and a Warner kick made the score 14-3.

In the fourth and deciding quarter, the Badgers took a Hoosier punt on their own 28 and four plays later had moved the ball past mid-field on the running of fullback Wayne Todd. Todd carried the ball seven times on the drive, the last play ending up on the Indiana 7. Todd was hurt however, on the play and had to leave the game. Indiana held, and the score remained 14-3.

Indiana was unable to move the ball down field, and Wisconsin got the ball back on its own 37. With senior Gale Buccairelli running for 33 yards in four plays, Wisconsin had the ball on the Indiana two. On the third down, the Hoosier defense stacked Buccairelli up at the line of scrimmage for no gain. On the fourth down play, Boyajian kept the ball and moved to his right, stumbling and sliding into the end zone for a Wisconsin score, and it was 14-9 Indiana. The Badgers would go for two hoping to make it a 3 point deficit. However, tight end Bill Fritz, who had already caught four big passes on the day, could not control a one handed catch that would have moved the Badgers to within a field goal. With the incomplete pass, the score remained 14-9 in favor of the Hoosiers with 3:36 left in the game. Time was running out on the Badgers, as Wisconsin tried an onside kick that failed to go the required 10 yards. Indiana took over on the Wisconsin 44.

49

Terry Cole #48 was a key blocker out of the backfield for Isenbarger #17.
Indiana University Archives (Wisconsin67-1393.12)

The Hoosiers were stopped on 4 plays and an Isenbarger punt went off the side of his foot out of bounds on the Wisconsin 34. There was just 1:28 left for the Badgers to score or IU to hold. During their final drive, Wisconsin converted a third or fourth down three times. A Boyajian pass to Bucciarell for 5, to Fritz for 30, and to Tom McCauley for 19 yards, put the ball at the IU 10. McCauley was unable to get out of bounds to stop the clock, so Boyajian threw a pass out of bounds to stop the clock at 15 seconds. The penalty on the out of bounds pass cost the Badgers 5 yards to the 15. A 5 yard swing pass to Dick Schumitsch got back the yardage, but cost valuable seconds, so Boyajian quickly set the last play in motion. A desperation throw into the end zone intended for Reddick, sailed out of the end zone.

Hoosiers celebrate homecoming win over the Badgers.
Indiana University Archives (Wisconsin67-1395.4)

The snow flurries coming down seemed to change to confetti, as pandemonium broke out in the end zone and in the stands. Alumni and students alike broke out in a chorus of Back Home Again in Indiana. The Hoosiers had been out-gained in every category, except the one that counted the most, for the scoreboard read Indiana 14, Wisconsin 9. The Hoosiers remained the only unbeaten Big Ten team, sharing the top spot in the Big Ten with Purdue and Minnesota.

FIRST DOWNS	IU	WISC
Total	17	20
Rushing	11	11
Passing	3	9
Penalty	3	0
RUSHING		
Rushes	55	48
Yards Gained	245	182
Yards Lost	47	15
Net Rushing Yardage	198	167

FORWARD PASSING

Attemped	12	37
Completed	3	15
Intercepted	2	2
Net Yards Passing	70	168

TOTAL PLAYS

(Rushing and Passes)	67	85

TOTAL NET YARDS

	268	335

PUNTING

Punts	7	6
Average Yards	29	39
Blocked	0	0

KICK RETURNS

Punts Returned	4	5
Punt Returned Yardage	14	47
Kickoff Returns	2	2
Kickoff Return Yards	18	34

INTERCEPTION RETURNS

Returned	2	2
Return Yards	11	51

FUMBLES

Fumbles	2	0
Fumbles Lost	1	0

PENALTIES

Penalties	1	8
Yards Penalized	15	93

Chapter 9

Indiana vs. Michigan State
November 11, 1967

Duffy's Revenge

Down to the last three games of the season, Hoosier fans could smell the roses all the way from Pasadena, California. Wins over Michigan State, Minnesota, and Purdue were all that were needed to give Indiana its first trip to the Rose Bowl ever, and only it's second Big Ten Football Championship. Wins over Purdue and Minnesota, teams that shared the top spot with IU in the Big Ten at 4-0, and Michigan State, the two time defending Big Ten Champ, was indeed a daunting task.

Entering the Michigan State game, IU was ranked sixth in both the AP & UPI polls, right behind number 5 Purdue. Several IU faithful would make the trip for the

John Isenbarger
Courtesy: IU Athletic Department
(967-0126)

1:30 p.m. clash before 71,023 fans at East Lansing. Over 5,000 paid $2.00 each to go to the new IU field house, the home of the Hurrying Hoosier basketball team, to watch a closed circuit TV broadcast of the game. The field house, where the legendary Coach Branch McCracken had coached his last game against Purdue, where the splendid splinter, Jimmy Rayl, had lit up the

53

Spartan basketball team for a Big Ten record 56 points, gathered over 5,000 fans to watch the Cardiac Kids of John Pont inch ever closer to a Big Ten Football Championship and a Rose Bowl appearance. So here they were, on November 11, Veteran's Day 1967. If basketball was indeed a religion in Indiana, at least for this season, it was the King James Version and the Hoosier Football Team was the Good News for Modern Man.

In the late fall of 1966, the number one ranked Spartans visited Bloomington, winning 37-19. Michigan State finished the season 7-0 in the Big Ten and 9-0-1 overall. Michigan State rolled into Memorial Stadium, not only winning the game, but inflicting injury upon injury to the Hoosier team, decimating it for the following week's trip to West Lafayette. Injured IU players included top receiver, Bill Couch, and defenseman, Kevin Duffy, with an injured spleen. The Spartans play was deemed so dirty by the Hoosier faithful that many had stayed after to boo and shout at the Spartan players as they boarded their bus to leave the stadium. (Being an impetuous junior high student, I even went down to the Michigan State locker room doors, pounding on them and challenging them to come out. Thank goodness no players took me up on that proposition.)

This was a trophy game for the Hoosiers who would try to bring home the Old Brass Spittoon. This Cinderella Hoosier Team of 1967 had walked a tightrope all season between victory and defeat. Winning their first seven games by margins of 2,3,4,5,7,13, and of course the 35 point blowout at Arizona. It mattered little to a Spartan team that returned Bob Apisa, Jimmy Raye, and Dwight Lee. Lee was Michigan State's leading rusher averaging 4.2 yards per carry and fullback, Apisa, was right behind him averaging 4.1 yards. Quarterback Raye had completed 33 of 76 passes and rushed for 158 yards. The Spartans were a 7 point favorite at game time.

The weather was wet and chilly. The play started out as ugly as the weather with both teams having 3 turnovers on the afternoon. Michigan State drew first blood in the second quarter as Charles Bailey recovered a Gonso pitch-out on the Indiana 7. The Hoosiers held firm for 3 downs, but a Pruiett 24 yard field goal kick before halftime gave the Spartans a 3-0 lead going into the locker room.

The Hoosiers came back in the third quarter. Gonso completed two bullet passes and then rushed in the end zone for a one yard score, and a Kornowa kick gave the Hoosiers the lead at 7-3 following the seventy yard drive. After a botched punt return put the Hoosiers with their backs to the wall on their own one, right tackle, George Chatlos engulfed Gonso on the one and threw him back into the end zone for a safety. Gonso, arguing in a style befitting the lawyer he would become, lost his case and the score stood at Indiana 7, Michigan State 5. The situation went from bad to worse as Michigan State received the free kick after the safety. Following a 14 yard penalty, the ball on the 32, Dwight Lee went in from the 4 and the Spartans lead 11-7. A pass from Wedenmeyer to Brenner gave Michigan State a two point conversion and the Spartans lead 13-7.

In the fourth, and deciding quarter, Indiana took over after a punt on their own 31. Sophomore halfback, John Isenbarger, returned to the game after being slammed down in the second quarter and shaken up again on the second half kick-off. Forty years later, center, Harold Mauro, would say, "Thank God for John Isenbarger!"

Iso sprinted for 12 yards on the first play of the drive. The next play Cole rush for three. Gonso hit Isenbarger for 15 and ran for 1 himself. Isenbarger carried for 14 more yards, and Cole picked up another 4. Indiana went back to Isenbarger for 13 more followed by another 3 by Cole. The Hoosier fans began to believe the Cardiac Kids might just do it again.

On this day, Mr. Cardiac wore #17 and went by the name of Isenbarger. With 13 yards to go to pay dirt, Gonso pitched wide right to Isenbarger who ran around the right side into the end zone for the tying score. All that was left was the conversion kick. Nearly 40 years later, Mauro would say, "I was so nervous. I had to get the snap just right." He did, and Dave Kornowa's kick was good. The Hoosiers lead 14-13, and it remained to be seen if they could hang on to win game number 8.

"After Iso scored, they threw a pass and our coaches worked really well on preparing us and I anticipated where the pass was going to be. I intercepted the ball and the guy drug me out of bounds, and that was the ball game," Ken Kacqmarek recalls of his last second interception of a Jimmy Raye pass.

The victory gave the Hoosiers possession of the Old Brass Spittoon, but there was one more tobacco related story of note in that game. Senior center, Harold Mauro, recalled, "There were not a whole lot of rules about what happened on the field in those days. There was chewing tobacco, you would get bit, just a little of everything would go on. I was the center and just before I would snap the ball for an extra point or punt, the guy lined up right across from me would spit tobacco juice on my hands. I showed the ump and he said to me come on, be tough, this is football. I said alright, so I told my two up backs on a punt one time, I'm going to stand this guy up and I want you to help me knock him down. When we got him down, I took my hand, and just rubbed the tobacco juice in his face and he complained to the umpire, who said to him, come on, it's football, just play the game." Years later Mauro said, "Maybe I should have gotten the brass spittoon!"

Kacqmarek, remembering the game said, "When we played Michigan State, I always knew it was going to be kind of a war, for me it always was. We had played against the same offensive line for 3 straight years. Kevin Duffy lost his spleen against Michigan State in 1966. I can remember him in the locker room before the game. He was kind of thinking about the game. He was so ready, he was going to do some damage for what happened last year. For some reason, I was really ready to play. It was one of the best games I ever had at IU, although we gave up 13, we really shut them out. I will never forget, they had first and goal on the 5 or 7 yard line, we blitzed one way and then we blitzed the other way. Then a crossing blitz and they were 4th and 9 and I'll never forget Jimmy Raye saying to one of his linemen, 'What the hell are you guys doing?' This guy looks at him and says, 'We know they are coming, we just don't know where.' We were laughing because we were just selling out every time just hoping they couldn't figure out where we were coming from. They ended up kicking a field goal and we had life."

John Isenbarger recalled with pride that Michigan State was especially hard to beat at East Lansing. The Hoosier's sophomore class could boast upon graduation that the Indiana Hoosiers had defeated the Michigan State Spartans three years in a row at East Lansing. Duffy's revenge would continue.

Indiana's win coupled with Purdue's trouncing of Minnesota 41-12 put the Hoosiers and Boilermakers at the top of the Big Ten standing with 5-0 records, and with just two games remaining. To quote Sonny and Cher, "...and the beat goes on."

FIRST DOWNS	IU	MSU
Total	21	9
Rushing	13	5
Passing	7	4
Penalty	1	0
RUSHING		
Rushes	62	43
Yards Gained	258	142
Yards Lost	61	20
Net Rushing Yardage	197	122
FORWARD PASSING		
Attemped	18	18
Completed	9	5
Intercepted	3	1
Net Yards Passing	130	54
TOTAL PLAYS		
(Rushing and Passes)	80	61
TOTAL NET YARDS	327	176
PUNTING		
Punts	4	7
Average Yards	44.5	41
Blocked	0	0
KICK RETURNS		
Punts Returned	3	4
Punt Returned Yardage	-13	42
Kickoff Returns	3	3
Kickoff Return Yards	32	50

INTERCEPTION RETURNS

Returned	1	3
Return Yards	2	18

FUMBLES

Fumbles	2	2
Fumbles Lost	2	0

PENALTIES

Penalties	5	8
Yards Penalized	65	85

Chapter 10

Indiana vs. Minnesota
November 18, 1967
A Half Step Off

November 18 took the Hoosiers to Minneapolis to face the 6-2 Gophers. A win and the Hoosiers would not only be 9-0, but assured of going to Pasadena on January 1st and making their very first appearance in the grand daddy of all the bowls, The Rose Bowl. The Hoosiers were coming off a difficult and inspiring 14-13 win over the Michigan State Spartans while the Gophers had been humbled by Purdue 41-12. All signs pointed to a favorable outcome, or so the Hoosier faithful hoped. Pont warned that Minnesota was the biggest, toughest team that his Hoosier squad had faced all year. The Minnesota defense outweighed the Hoosier offensive line by an average of 20 pounds.

The game would again be shown via closed circuit broadcast in the field house and all six thousand tickets had long been sold out. The game would be played on a beautiful, but very windy fall afternoon. The Hoosiers came into this game as a seven point favorite, but it was clear from the outset that this would be a long, hard fought affair.

A scoreless affair in the first quarter, both teams resembled heavyweight prize fighters landing punches, but no knockouts during the early stages of this crucial game. The first time the Gophers had possession of the football, they marched down the field, rushing almost non-stop until an ill-advised Wilson pass was intercepted by linebacker, Kevin Duffy, on the Hoosier 34. Four plays later, defensive end, Del Jessen, ripped the ball out of would be runner, Harry Gonso's hand and Noel Jenke recovered on the Indiana 40.

Six plays into the new Minnesota drive, Wilson overthrew his intended receiver, Carter, and into the waiting hands of IU's Nate Cunningham, only to have the ball slip through his hands to the ground for an incomplete pass. Given a second chance on a fourth

59

and two, Wilson faked a hand off and raced around the right side behind 250 pound right tackle, John Williams, and 245 pound junior right guard, Dick Enderle, into the end zone for one of his record setting 4 rushing touchdowns for the Minnesota quarterback from Lawton, Oklahoma. Williams and Enderle were a battering ram steam rolling the left side of Indiana's defensive line. Minnesota's running attack on this day included John Winternute rushing for 135 yards in 23 attempts, followed by Wilson's 118 yards in 20 attempts and Carter's 94 yards in 19 carries.

In the second period, Indiana was able to move the ball and it looked as if they were going to answer Minnesota's touchdown with one of their own only to have Gonso's 15 yard scoring strike to Butcher called back on an ineligible receiver penalty. Gonso ran past the line of scrimmage to nullify the pass attempt. The Hoosiers tried a 42 yard field goal, only to miss and go down at half by a score of 7-0.

Indiana opened the 3rd quarter by moving the ball 76 yards in 15 plays. Isenbarger carried the ball 5 times for 29 yards and Gonso ran 5 times for 21 yards. Gonso, spreading the defense, hit Gage with a 10 yard strike and Butcher for a 22 yard catch as the Hoosier offense looked full throttle. Gonso would finish the drive by going over right tackle with a keeper that gave Indiana its first touchdown of the day. Kornowa's kick made it 7-7 with 8:53 to go in the third quarter.

Indiana seemed to be following an all too familiar script for the 4,500 faithful who came to Minneapolis and the thousands of fans watching on closed circuit television in the field house and listening at home on the radio. One of those young fans listening on the radio remembers yelling at the radio when the officials' whistle went against his beloved Hoosiers. He was certain it was an errant call, for of course he could see the play so much better on the radio than the officials at the game. Such was the devotion and love this team came to elicit.

Hoosier fans were even undaunted when Wilson scored his second touchdown of the day with 24 seconds left in the third quarter. Jim Sniadecki's block of the extra point attempt kept the score at 13-7. Hoosier fans everywhere seemed to smile, wink, and nod to each other "Here we go again, it's the fourth quarter and we're down 13-7. It is time for the Cardiac Kids to pull out another game from the jaws of defeat."

Taking the kickoff, Al Gage returned the ball 7 yards. Gonso and Isenbarger moved the ball down to the Minnesota 26 on eight plays and Indiana looked poised to score and take their first lead of the game. On a fourth and 9, Gonso running the patented Hoosier option, instead of pitching the ball to a waiting Isenbarger who had fullback Cole ready to block, kept the ball instead and ran down the sideline to pick up 5 yards, 4 yards short of the first down. Minnesota then marched down field and Wilson ran into the end zone only to be met by a jarring tackle that knocked the ball loose back to the Indiana 10 with Hoosier, Dave Kornowa, recovering the fumble. The officials however, ruled that Wilson was in and that Minnesota had scored again to make the score 19-7 with 7:20 remaining. Minnesota's kick-off hung high in the wind and Indiana's Jade Butcher misjudging the ball, waiting on a bounce that did not come his way. Minnesota's Dennis Hale recover the ball on the IU 23. It was Gopher football again.

Jade would later shake his head and stare into space saying, "I should have had that ball. When I realized it wasn't coming directly to me, I ran as fast as I could, only to see Minnesota recover the kickoff." Shaking his head and still staring, Jade just said, "I should have had it. If I get that ball, we could win and stay undefeated."

Kaczmarek said, "We were just off, the plays we made at Michigan State, at Minnesota we just didn't make. On one option play a player got my leg and the quarterback was able to turn the corner. The week before, I would have creamed him. We were just a half step off all game."

Four plays later, on a fourth down pass, Wilson's throw was knocked down by Kornowa only to have it fall to Charles Sanders who was running behind the play. He scrambled for a 17 yard touchdown play; the successful kick making it 26-7. The final Minnesota touchdown would come when on a Gonso pitch missed Isenbarger and was recovered on the Indiana 23 by Bill Laakso. Seven plays later, Wilson recorded his record setting fourth touchdown on a one yard run, to make the final score a crushing 33-7.

Hoosier fans everywhere cried; yet, they were waiting for their teams' return to Bloomington. No one had given up. There was still one more game; Purdue, a game that on many occasions defined the season. This time it would define a season like no other.

FIRST DOWNS	IU	MN
Total	18	21
Rushing	13	17
Passing	3	3
Penalty	2	1
RUSHING		
Rushes	44	67
Yards Gained	223	355
Yards Lost	48	29
Net Rushing Yardage	175	326
FORWARD PASSING		
Attemped	15	13
Completed	4	6
Intercepted	0	1
Net Yards Passing	66	54
TOTAL PLAYS		
(Rushing and Passes)	59	80
TOTAL NET YARDS	241	380
PUNTING		
Punts	3	3
Average Yards	46	32
Blocked	0	0
KICK RETURNS		
Punts Returned	0	1
Punt Returned Yardage	0	18
Kickoff Returns	6	1
Kickoff Return Yards	81	17

INTERCEPTION RETURNS

Returned	1	0
Return Yards	0	0

FUMBLES

Fumbles	3	1
Fumbles Lost	3	1

PENALTIES

Penalties	6	9
Yards Penalized	56	115

Chapter 11

November 19-24, 1967

Preparing for Purdue

The Hoosiers arrived back in Bloomington after a very long, quiet trip following the heart breaking loss to Minnesota. The police escort leading the team turned toward the new field house as Pont announced to the players that this building was their next destination of the night. The players began to wonder if after the events of the day they were going to be practicing in the field house with all that sawdust. Further disappointment began to set in.

When they walked into the field house, much to their surprise and delight, the field house was full of fans thanking them for what

The Old Oaken Bucket
Courtesy: IU Athletics

they had accomplished so far and providing support for the big game coming up against Purdue.

Pont went to the podium and addressed both the crowd of supporters and the team, announcing to everyone, "Tonight, we just beat Purdue!" "And I meant it," Pont elaborated almost 40 years later, "the outpouring of support was unbelievable."

The coaching staff went to work on the psyche of the team. They had a dinner for the players, a mock celebration of the team going to the Rose Bowl. Of course, they had not won the right to represent the Big Ten yet. The point was clear: they still had work to do. The players and the coaching staff resolved to put the Minnesota game behind them and concentrate on the contest before them, the Purdue game.

The weather in Bloomington reflected the mood of the team after Saturday's loss. It was an overcast, gloomy, cold, crummy week. Monday featured the annual Purdue bonfire and the burning of "Jawn" Purdue. At this event, some students would appear with the Old Oaken Bucket that had been taken from the Purdue campus. In practice Monday, the team began to focus on the game at hand.

Ken Kaczmarek recalled that, "Monday, Pont got all the seniors together before practice and said, 'Ken you want to go to Hawaii to play in the Hula Bowl? They want you to come and be a part of the game.' Of course I said yes, I would love to. Coach then went to some of the other seniors and asked them about various other bowls that had invited them to play and this made us all feel real good.

"The coaches then got the whole team together and said that you have a great opportunity here to do something very special. Don't think that you can't beat Purdue because you can and with our help you will. Tuesday, we started to say what are we thinking about here, we really can do this. Wednesday was a great practice, Minnesota was gone by now.

"That year the Purdue game was after Thanksgiving, so we practiced in the morning on Thursday. Coach Pont had some of us to his house and Dr. Bomba had others to his house so we split the squad. We just ate and sat around talking and watching football, and by Friday when we went out to break a sweat, everyone knew we were going to win."

The team went to McCormick's Creek on Friday, like always, to get away, view films and prepare for Saturday's game. Jade Butcher recalled his roommate, " T Bear, Terry Cole, was a little down that night, sharing a certain sadness that it was his last game at IU, and when he had arrived at Indiana as a freshman, he had hopes of playing professional football. He feared that because of his reduced role in carrying the ball that the flame on that dream had gone out." Jade said years later, "I never shared this with anyone and I am no soothsayer, but I just had a feeling, and I shared it with Terry that 'Terry you're going to have the best game of your career tomorrow.' I just knew that Terry was going to come up huge." On Saturday, Jade was as sure with his hands as with his prediction whenever the football was thrown close to him.

Gonso shared that as gloomy as the week had been, Saturday was just the opposite, "It was warm and sunny. In fact, I was to return punts on that day, and it was so bright that in practice before the game, I lost one punt in the sun so badly it hit me on the helmet." The week starting on Sunday that looked so gloomy, had turned into this beautiful sunny fall day, and the sun on that afternoon would shine brightest on the Hoosier side of the field.

Bill Murphy

Chapter 12

Indiana vs. Purdue
November 25, 1967

The Ultimate Bucket Game

Snoopy knows best.
Indiana University Archives (Purdue67-1476.11)

Remember the number 60, for numbers within the sixties seemed to play an important part in the annual rivalry game between long time foes, Indiana and Purdue. The first three games played in this series in 1891, '92, and '93. All saw Purdue defeat IU by scores of 60-0, 68-0, and 64-0. On the 64th meeting of these two schools, IU had beaten Purdue 12 to 7 on a record 92 yard pass interception by junior Marv Woodson, which brought the bucket back to Bloomington for only the second time in 15 seasons. On this beautiful November day, the number 63 would be the most important.

Going into this game, the bucket had resided in West Lafayette for the past four years. The bucket however, had been missing from its burglar proof case for over a month, having been taken from its spot of honor on the Purdue campus by a group of Indiana students who had scaled the side of a building, entered through a window, and picked the lock, taking the bucket back to Bloomington. On Monday night before Saturday's game, with the traditional burning of John Purdue at the bonfire, the adventurous students ran out during the pep rally, with the bucket filled with roses. Tuesday the bucket was returned to the desk of Purdue Athletic Director, Red Mackey, who was unaware of its absence. When Purdue coach, Jack Mollenkophf, heard of the theft, his response was, "That's the only way they can get the bucket."

The verbal shots had been fired. The game of words, partying, and tradition were on. Saturday's game would be one of the biggest bucket games of all time. It was the first time in the 77 year history of the rivalry that both teams would come into the game with identical 8 and 1 records. One had to go back 22 years when in 1945, Purdue entered the game with a record of 7-2 having lost only to Northwestern and Michigan, while Indiana entered the game 8-0-1 with its only blemish a 7-7 tie to Northwestern in its second game of the season, to find a game of equal magnitude. This time a Rose Bowl appearance was on the line.

*Mike Krivshia #35 and Al Schmidt # 74 lead the team onto the field. **Indiana University Archives (Purdue67-1476.9)***

For the Hoosiers, a victory meant a share of the Big Ten Championship, while for Purdue; a victory would give them their first undisputed Big Ten title in 38 years. A win would probably give IU a top 10 finish nationally for the first time since finishing fourth in 1945. While Purdue, coming into the game was ranked third nationally, and could finish with its highest ranking ever, previous high being fifth in 1944. This had been an improbable year, to say the least, for the Hoosiers. Indiana had come into the season having lost quarterback Frank Stavroff, all Big Ten offensive guard, Tom Schuette, center Bob Van Pelt, and splitend Bill Couch., who had enrolled in medical school. Stavroff held the Big Ten single game passing record of 316 yards against Michigan State in 1966. Pont had molded 27 returning lettermen and a group of charismatic sophomores, into a team of undaunted, never say die, players ready to take on the world; and so they had.

The game had long been a sellout, and a record crowd of 52,770 would witness a game no one would soon forget. Fans called long lost friends that might have an extra ticket. Favors were cashed in, one fan even boasted after the game that he had crashed into the game by telling the usher the guy behind him had the ticket and then running like crazy once he was inside. On a personal note, I had not missed a game all year as a regular knothole kid, but my parents were using our two season tickets so I was left to figure out how to watch the game on my own. The trees at each end of the stadium were not very big at the time, so one could stand behind the fence and peer in, to see the

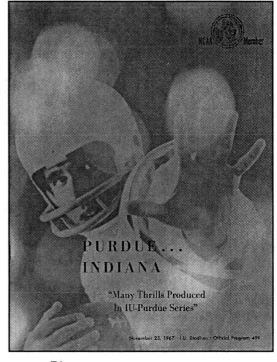

PURDUE...
INDIANA

"Many Thrills Produced
In IU-Purdue Series"

November 25, 1967 · I.U. Stadium · Official Program 49¢

71

game fairly well from each end zone. This method was probably best for a Jr. High boy to view the game as I was able to go from end zone to end zone depending upon Indiana's field position. The moving about was helpful to a young lad too nervous to sit down anyway.

The program that day featured a football player in red cradling a ball and holding out his left arm as if to stiff arm an opponent. The quote read "Many Thrills Produced in IU-Purdue Series". The program did not lie. Terry Cole entered the game carrying the ball 94 times without losing a yard all season. Leory Keyes had gained 872 yards for a 6.7 yards per carry average. Fullback Perry Williams had gained 622 yards a 4.2 average, and Columbus' Mike Phipps, who had chosen Purdue over Indiana, had completed 107 passes for 1,659 yards and 11 touchdowns. Isenbarger and Cole led IU in rushing with 518 and 501 yards respectively. Gonso had completed 58 passes for 820 yards and 7 touchdowns. Indiana was pronounced a 14 point underdog. The Swami out of Chicago said Purdue would win 21 to 14.

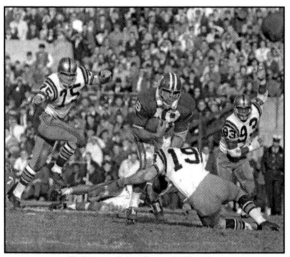

Cole running through Purdue.
Indiana University Archives (Purdue67-1524.4)

On the very first series of downs, defensive end Tom Bilunas knocked the ball out of quarterback Phipps hands, and Indiana recovered on the Purdue 44. Indiana could not move the ball on that possession, but after an exchange of punts, fullback Terry Cole took the first hand-off and rushed up the middle for 42 yards to the Purdue 9. Then Gonso on a third and 7 on the 7 found Jade Butcher over the middle for the games first score. Leory Keyes had told Butcher that he wasn't going to catch anything. Jade just said watch me. Keyes just happen to be out of the game and standing along the sidelines watching as Jade caught the touchdown pass holding it high for all to see, as was his tradition. A Dave Kornowa kick was good, and Indiana led 7 to 0 with just 7 minutes and 26 seconds into this game.

Purdue being summarily kicked in the face by IU's first score, took the Hoosier kick off and marched 85 yards in 10 plays to score, tying the game. During the drive, Phipps completed 3 passes to Jim Beirne for 38 yards. Fullback Perry Williams ran through the middle for a 9 yard touchdown. The first quarter ended in a 7-7 tie.

Pont directing the team.
Indiana University Archives (Purdue67-1477.4)

73

In the second quarter, both teams seemed to do everything possible to give the game away. First IU's Gonso threw an interception to defensive back Bob Corby from Wilmette, Ill. All-American Leory Keyes dropped a long pass at the Indiana 5, and Purdue was forced to punt. IU would again turn the ball over, as Gonso was intercepted again by Corby and Purdue was again presented another golden opportunity to score.

Keyes fumbled, this time on a fourth and 3, and Indiana's Cal Snowden recovered at the 37. Ken Kaczmarek talking about the Indiana defense of Keyes, said "We hit Keyes so hard 4 times, one by Kornowa, one by Cunningham, one by Sniadecki, and one of the tackles where the helmet hit into his ribs, by the end of the game, that poor guy could hardly pick up his arms. He had a hard time catching the ball, because he just couldn't pick up his arms."

Crusan #78, Duffy #37 and Kornowa #14 in on the stop.
Indiana University Archives (Purdue67-1524.12)

This time Indiana drove 63 yards, there is that number 63, in nine plays, including a Gonso to Isenbarger 20 yard pass play all the way to the Purdue 2. Fullback Mike Krivoshia ran in from the 2, and Indiana lead 13 to 7 following an unsuccessful Indiana kick.

Krivoshia scoring TD to put IU up 13-7.
Indiana University Archives (Purdue67-1475/20)

Harold Mauro later recalled no one wanted to tackle Krivoshia in practice, "He was a bull, in fact during the Purdue game, he got a penalty called on him that I had never heard of before. He was called for a roughing the defense penalty, he just didn't hear the whistle on the play, and he kept going using his forearms to drive and knock people off of him. He was just so tough, he would hurt people."

Purdue took the kickoff and again marched down field, only to have Phipps 5 yard pass to Bob Dillingham result in a fumble. Indiana's Harold Dunn recovered the ball at the Indiana 29. With Indiana in control of the football on a third and 2, Purdue brought its linebackers to the line and its backs to cover the flanks. Indiana had expected this, and had put in a play designed to go to the fullback Cole. The senior from Mitchell, Indiana rambled 63 yards for Indiana's third and last touchdown. Jade's predictions was coming a reality. The half ended with Indiana in the lead 19 to 7.

In the second half, after both teams had exchanged punts, the Boilermakers ended up with the ball on the Indiana 46. Keyes had runs of 13 and 22 yards, and with the ball on the Indiana 2 fullback Williams dove over to make the score 19 to 13. Baltzell's twenty-fifth kick of the season, a Big Ten record, made the score 19 to 14 Indiana.

The Hoosier fans had 15 minutes of football left before they could breathe again. On the first play of the forth quarter, Indiana relinquished possession of the ball on a punt, and for the next eight and a half minutes, Purdue taking over on their own 20, would march 76 yards in 20 plays. Purdue was on the Hoosier 4 poised to score the go ahead touchdown, and take the lead in the contest. A Purdue fan in a crowd of Hoosier friends stood up and yelled as loud as he could, "There go those roses!" As those fateful words came out of his mouth, both Harold Dunn and Ken Kaczmarek

Kaczmarek solo tackle.
Indiana University Archives
(967-1478.15)

76

met fullback Williams head on with jarring tackles that caused the most famous fumble in Indiana football history.

Ken Kaczmarek remembered it this way, "What really happened was that, what we really worked on as linebackers was that if a hole opened up, you had better fill it because something would be coming. I moved in kind of like attacking in I formation, in that type of situation you sometimes really don't know who has the ball. Harold Dunn and I just hit Perry at the same time, and he dropped the ball, and it just rolled around on the ground. It rolled through Duffy's legs toward the end zone, then Mike Baughman jumped on the ball, that kind of just sealed the deal."

Indiana was unable to move the ball, and Pont called on Isenbarger to punt the ball. John Isenbarger, as he was running out, said jokingly to Pont, "Do you want me to kick or run with the ball?" Isenbarger said later that standing there in his end zone, he said to himself "You know you have got to get a pretty good kick off here," and he did. Isenbarger boomed the ball out of the end zone 63 yards, over friend Tim Foley's head. Foley was able to recover the ball and run it back 7 yards to the Indiana 40. Years later, several Indiana players would talk about that kick, and share that there was some thought to taking a safety and gaining the opportunity to have a free kick. The defense was playing so well, the decision was made to allow John to just punt the ball, and what a great idea it turned out to be.

Purdue gained one first down, but Phipps was not able to convert a fourth down pass play, and Indiana took possession on the Purdue 46. Indiana again unable to move the football, would punt the ball away, giving Purdue one last chance with 60 seconds left. Phipps passed the ball to Jim Kirkpatrick for 27 yards, then ran for 12, before passing to Beirne for 11. The ball was now on the Indiana 30, with only 14 seconds remaining. Phipps completed a pass to Baltzell to the 23, as time ran out. For the second time in this game, time had run out on Purdue, as the ball rested on the Indiana 23. This time the game was over. Indiana had tried on the glass slipper and it did indeed fit.

the Bucket victory, and a Rose Bowl trip.
Courtesy: IU and Harold Mauro

Purdue had out gained Indiana 426 yards to 344. Purdue had 26 first downs to Indiana's 15. The Boilermakers had fumbled the ball 4 times to the Hoosier's none. Most importantly, the final on the Hoosier Scoreboard read, Indiana 19 Purdue 14. Indiana had won the bucket, the Big Ten Championship, and a trip to Pasadena.

Senior fullback Terry Cole, fulfilling the McCormick's Creek predictions of roommate Jade Butcher, had his greatest day as a Hoosiers running back, rushing for 155 yards and one touchdown. Gonso had out dueled Phipps completing 9 of 20 passes for 111 yards and a touchdown. Phipps had passed for 11 of 28 on the day for 141 yards.

The headlines for The Bloomington Tribune on Sunday, November 26, said in black and red, "We Did It! We're Going! IU Upsets Purdue, 19-14, Gets Bid". As for that number 63, there was Cole's 63 yard touchdown run, Isenbarger's 63 yard punt with just over 6 minutes left, Indiana's second touchdown drive that went for 63 yards, and finally there were 63 plays from scrimmage for IU.

If history is a series of cause and events, events and results, then the results of that November day in 1967 were that IU would make the Rose Bowl. Indiana had gained a share of the Big Ten Championship with Purdue and Minnesota. The Old Oaken Bucket had returned to Bloomington, this time legally. Indiana had beaten Purdue for the first time in 20 years at home, and for the first time in the new Memorial Stadium. The Hoosiers had defeated the greatest offense in Big Ten history. Indiana had recorded 9 wins in a season for only the second time in school history, and finished fourth in the AP and sixth in the UPI regular season poll. It was truly a magical season, a season that would continue on January 1 with the Rose Bowl.

FIRST DOWNS	IU	PU
Total	15	26
Rushing	7	18
Passing	7	8
Penalty	1	0
RUSHING		
Rushes	42	61

Yards Gained	260	313
Yards Lost	27	39
Net Rushing Yardage	233	274
FORWARD PASSING		
Attemped	21	29
Completed	9	12
Intercepted	2	0
Net Yards Passing	111	152
TOTAL PLAYS		
(Rushing and Passes)	63	90
TOTAL NET YARDS	344	426
PUNTING		
Punts	7	5
Average Yards	40	40
Blocked	0	0
KICK RETURNS		
Punts Returned	3	4
Punt Returned Yardage	39	25
Kickoff Returns	2	3
Kickoff Return Yards	27	75
INTERCEPTION RETURNS		
Returned	0	2
Return Yards	0	18
FUMBLES		
Fumbles	0	5
Fumbles Lost	0	4
PENALTIES		
Penalties	4	3
Yards Penalized	35	40

Chapter 13

Terry Hoeppner
A Rose Bowl Wish

Coach Terry Hoeppner at his first IU press conference.
Indiana Football

The thirteenth chapter is dedicated to Coach Terry Hoeppner, who like Coach Pont, came to Indiana after a very successful career at Miami of Ohio. Coach Hoeppner brought an attitude that was contagious to the entire state. He was himself a big fan of Indiana University and the '67 team. He used the '67 team as an example of what he wanted Indiana University to become again.

Coach Heppner's mantra was to play 13, which meant IU would go to a bowl. For this reason, I have dedicated the thirteenth chapter to him. Coach was very fond of the poem Don't Quit, and those who knew him knew also he lived it. We thank Coach Hoeppner for all he brought to IU, and he brought much. He will be missed, but like the '67 team, his legacy will live forever.

DON'T QUIT
Author Unknown

When things go wrong as they sometimes will,
And the road you are trudging seems all up hill;
When the funds are low and the debts are high,
And you want to smile but you have to sigh;
When care is pressing you down a bit,
Rest if you must, but don't you quit.
For life is strange with its twists and turns,
As every one of us sometimes learns;
But many a coward turns about
When he might have won had he stuck it out.
But he learns too late when the night comes down
How close he was to the golden crown.
Victory is defeat turned inside out,
The silver tint of the clouds of doubt.
You will never know how near you are -
It may be close when it seems afar.
So stick to the fight when you are hardest hit;
It is when things seem worst that you must not quit.

Indiana Football

Chapter 14

California Here We Come

Officially this was Indiana's first trip to the Rose Bowl, however unofficially, the Hoosiers had arrived back in January of 1874. In 1873, an organization of Indiana people met in the Indianapolis home of Dr. T B. Elliot hoping to plan an emigration to sunny California. They proceeded to buy land and begin a colonization of the area to be known as the Indiana Colony. Arriving on January 27, 1874 with an influx of other groups as well, Dr. Elliott changed his original thought of calling this area the Indiana Colony and instead used the Chippewa word Pasadena, which meant "valley between the hills" This time however, instead of arriving by horse, they arrived by the largest contingent of planes in Rose Bowl history.

The announcement was made on Saturday night, Indiana was indeed going to the Rose Bowl. The Cardiac Kids of Coach John Pont would represent Indiana University and the Big Ten in the Rose Bowl. The attention of the students, faculty, and fans would turn to sunny California, and how to get their tickets, plan their trip, and where to stay once they arrived. The entire United States would see the largest civilian air lift in the history of U.S aviation. The Hoosiers would take at least 35 chartered jets to sunny Pasadena and the Rose Bowl.

The 20 member staff of WIUS would start on November 26th holding a week long marathon to be the first in line for their Rose Bowl tickets. This 20 person crew headed up by Al Remy of Cordon, Indiana, would take two hour shifts and provide the campus with up to date Rose Bowl information. This information would come from a make shift shelter to help them maintain their first in line status. The rest of the student population began to line up after 9:30 pm on Sunday, November 27th, and by 1:00 a.m., more then 10 people had camped out on that very chilly November night. By Monday over 2,648 Rose Bowl receipts were given out. Students purchasing tickets were required to have a valid ID. Then according to Big Ten Policy, these students would be required to have the same ID in California as well, to pick up their tickets. The students were given a pink receipt card to be exchanged for a $3.50 refund, and a Rose Bowl ticket, at the IU ticket office, in the lobby of the of the Southern California Edison Co., located at the corner of 5th and Grand, from 9:00 am to 4 pm. on Dec 27th ,28th , and 29th. December 30th from 9am until noon would be the last day and time to pick up their tickets. The students could purchase their tickets from Monday to Wednesday 8:00 a.m. to 8:00 p.m., while the faculty and staff would purchase their tickets on Thursday and Friday from 8 to 8.

IU float in the Rose Bowl parade.
Indiana University Archives

The IU float would be called "The Greatest Adventure," and feature a huge block IU, with seven lovely co-eds in the front, and the Rose Bowl Stadium and giant roses in the rear of the float. A pep rally took place in the new fieldhouse on Tuesday, at 6:30 p.m., which was covered live by Channel 4. Bob Collins, a sports columnist for the Indianapolis Star, was Master of Ceremonies and the McNutt Crimsonaires led songs such as "California Here We Come" and "We've Got the Whole World in Our Hands" the latter which by now had become famous, as the theme song of this bunch of Hoosier football players. The first song had the lyrics changed to say:

Pasadena here we come,
Pump us up and watch us run.
We played 'em, we slayed 'em, we're number 1,
We'll beat you; defeat you, just before the final gun.
The Happy Hooligans are having fun,
Punt John, punt John, please don't run
Mind Coach Pont, the son-of-a-gun
Pasadena here we come.

This pep rally was the first, but there would be another in Pasadena at the International Plaza in the International Hotel, and a third, when the team returned on January 3, at the new fieldhouse.

IU President Herman B. Wells.
Indiana University Archives

IU asked and received permission to take a 50 man traveling squad to Pasadena, rather than the allowed 44 man squad. Southern California would become what it was supposed to become some 94 years ago, a colony of Hoosiers. The team itself left from Weir

Cook Airport in Indianapolis, on December 21st. They would board a Boeing 727 to go to Los Angeles. The Cardiac Kids arrived in Los Angeles, and the count down was on. Indiana would ready themselves for game eleven, the Rose Bowl, and prepare to represent Indiana University for the first time ever in a bowl game, and this was the granddaddy of all bowls, the Rose Bowl.

Chapter 15

Pre-Rose Bowl

Pont leads the team onto the LA tarmac. The Hoosiers have arrived.
Indiana University Archives

The 79th Rose Bowl would be Indiana's first experience representing the Big Ten in Pasadena. At the start of the '67 season, this seemed like such an unlikely event, yet as the season rolled on, the scent of roses grew stronger with each passing victory. The team did not learn of their fate until the evening after the Purdue game. Harold Mauro was at his apartment with many of the other players, when Coach Pont called and asked if any of the other players were there. Harold said yes, and Coach Pont said, "Well, tell them we're going to the Rose Bowl."

The party broke out and the fun began. Ken Kaczmarek said, "We didn't find out until about 7:30 that night, then the party started."

The team, coaches, administrators, and families left a rainy Bloomington on December 21st, for sunny California. At the Los Angeles Airport, they were greeted by the Rose Bowl Committee and the Rose Bowl Queen, Linda Strothen, who appropriately enough presented Coach Pont with a glass slipper.

The 79th Rose Bowl would be the first satellite television broadcast to Europe of a college football game. Coach Pont recalled, "I told the team that the Rose Bowl was their reward for the season. We want you to have a good time. We will practice in the morning on one day, and the afternoon the next, but the night will be yours. For 7 days, enjoy yourselves, there will be cars and drivers provided for groups of you players. We will let you do what you want at night. If you want to go to a disco and dance here or there or whatsoever, go. You must promise you are not going to get in trouble, no drinking, have a good time, then we're going to cut if off and get busy."

Doug Crusan recalled, "The Rose Bowl, boy that was special. We spent the week practicing; they showed you a really good time. It was a culmination of a great year. It was saying to us, you guys are good and you deserve this, and here's what you have got to do now. I will never forget the emotions I experienced on January 1, 1968 representing Indiana University and standing in the middle of the Rose Bowl before 102,000 people for the toss of the coin."

Harold Mauro remembered the players switching from high top shoes to low cut ones, "We knew we were going to be on TV, and we wanted to look good."

Pont recalled taking the team to the Passionate Fathers' Retreat, a monastery located in the foothills of the San Gabriel Mountains, just outside of Pasadena, "The players were in awe, many had never been in a monastery before. The dinners were great. It was so peaceful."

Jade Butcher would say, "This is quieter than McCormick's Creek." Pont remembered some players did get in trouble with him, as he found them climbing the mountains behind the monastery. The monastery would provide a getaway for the Hoosiers, who had enjoyed a trip to Disneyland, and a traditional dinner at the Big Ten Club of Southern California in the Hollywood Palladium with one of IU's most famous alums, Hoagy Carmichael.

The team met USC at the famous Los Angeles restaurant, Lawry's, for an eating contest. Indiana would eat 289 pounds of prime rib to USC's record 321 pounds. Mauro said, "We knew they were big right then and there." Captain, Crusan said, "You must remember though, we were on Pont's diet for speed. In '66 I think it would have been much closer." The team had experienced the well deserved rewards of a season to remember, as the game was about to unfold in the foothills of Southern California.

IU practicing in California. **Indiana University Archives**

Chapter 16

Indiana vs. University of Southern California
January 1, 1968
The Rose Bowl

Courtesy: Tournament of Roses Archive

Millions of people from around the world watched as the USC Trojans kicked to Indiana to begin the 79th Rose Bowl. Back home in Indiana, Hoosiers gathered with friends and family to watch IU's first ever appearance, while satellite coverage provided a bowl experience like no other to Europe.

John Isenbarger would field the kick-off at the seven and run the ball out to the Indiana 25 for an 18 yard gain, and Indiana would start their first Bowl game with possession of the football. As Harry Gonso stood under center, he barked out the count and took the snap. Rolling to his left, he gained 5 yards to the 30, as Indiana gained positive yardage in their first play from scrimmage. On the next play, Cole took the hand-off from Gonso and ran up the middle for 3 to the 33. Gonso would take the next snap, rolling to his right this time and rush for 7 to the 40 and an Indiana first down. Cole ran up the middle for two, followed by no gain as Gonso rolled to his left and misfired on a pass. On third and 8, Gonso would again roll left. However, this time, the pass was perfect and Gage would gather the ball in at the USC 44 for a second Indiana first down. Isenbarger would take the hand-off and be trapped for a one yard loss. Gonso then rolled out right and overthrew intended receiver Jade Butcher at the USC 20. With a third and 11, Gonso dropped back to pass. A huge rush by the USC defense chased him all the way back to the Indiana 37. Harry would get off an incomplete pass, with a flag thrown on the play. IU was penalized for offensive pass interference. Isenbarger fell back to punt on his

own 30. His kick would bounce all the way down to the USC 16, where the Trojans took over first and ten. Indiana's first series of possession, in their first bowl game had come to an end.

Indiana University Archives
(RoseBowlAerial971-0267)

In the stands, were not only the boosters, the faculty, and students of Indiana University, but family and friends of the team that had made the pilgrimage to Pasadena. For many family members, it was their first airplane flight, for others, it was their first civilian flight, as some had flown in military service. The Rose Bowl was a sea of red that January 1, 1968, with red and white pompoms waving everywhere. Signs were displayed throughout the stadium, some proclaiming the nomination of Pont for President. Other signs would encourage the Hoosiers to make Simpson part of everyone's breakfast, as they said squeeze O.J. Still other signs going with the Cinderella Theme, would acknowledge Indiana as everyone's Cinderella, while declaring the Cinderella Hoosiers wore brass knuckles. Many of the nine teams Indiana had beaten that season would concur that the IU defense did indeed hit as if they had brass knuckles.

Junior quarterback Steve Sogge, from Gardena, California, who came into the game with 71 completions on 144 attempts for 975 yards and 7 touchdowns, would pass to senior end, Earl McCullouch, for a first down on the Indiana 28. On the next play, junior running back, O.J. Simpson, ran a Sogge pitch down the right side of the field to the USC 40 only to have the play called back on a clipping call. The ball was now resting on the USC 22, and another run by O.J. off right tackle advanced the ball to the USC 35. Junior fullback Dan Scott from Pico Rivera, California, took the hand-off off left tackle out to the 39. Sogge threw to the senior end from Long Beach, Earl McCullouch, who caught the pass for a 10 yard gain all the way to the 49 for another first down. An illegal motion penalty took the ball back to the 44. USC's quarterback, Sogge, dropped back to pass and connected to senior Ron Drake from Pico Rivera, California, for a 19 yard pass play all the way down to the Indiana 37. Southern Cal's high powered offense that averaged over 24 points a game, was moving the ball on its first offensive series. Fullback Dan Scott went two yards on a quick hitter up the middle, then Simpson went off right tackle to the 20 for another first down. Sogge, on a quarterback sneak, went for three, down to the 17. Simpson, taking the hand-off, went off

93

left tackle down to the 11. Then USC came right back to Simpson off the right tackle, this time to the 7 and yet another first down. Simpson went up the middle down to the six. Scott hammered his way up the middle to the 2. USC finished off the 84 yard drive, with O.J. for the first touchdown of the game. The extra point was good, and USC lead 7-0 with 4:48 to go in the first quarter.

Southern California's second kick-off of the game was received by Isenbarger in the end zone. John ran the ball for a twenty-one yard gain out to the 21, and Indiana was ready to take over for the second time of the game. On Indiana's first play of the second possession, Gonso pitched right to Isenbarger to the 22. Gonso, on the second play of this series, kept the ball and went to the 27 for a five yard gain, only to lose the ball on a fumble that USC recovered.

Southern Cal tried for a quick hitter on the first play of its second possession. Sogge dropped back and passed into the end zone. The pass was incomplete, and it was second and ten. Sophomore Steve Dale took the hand-off and rambled 7 yards to the 20. Scott ran up the middle to the 14 for a first down, and USC was marching again. Scott, who was hammering the Indiana line as he battered his way down the field, ran off the right side to the five. Sogge would sneak to the 3, and USC would have another first down. Scott went down to the 2, but fumbled the ball into the end zone. It was recovered by Indiana's Mike Baughman and Indiana had prevented a quick USC touchdown to keep the score at USC 7 to Indiana 0.

Indiana's John Isenbarger took the hand-off from Gonso and ran to the right for 2 yards. Gonso rolled out and threw a perfect strike to Gage on the Indiana 33, and Indiana was beginning to march down field again. There had been those who doubted Indiana's ability to stay in a game against the powerful USC Trojans, but Indiana was demonstrating to all that they indeed belonged in this, the most prestigious of all bowl games. Mike Krivoshia rushed for 4 yards up the middle to the 37. Gonso would then try to complete a pass into USC territory only to get picked off by Southern Cal's junior defensive back, Jim Snow.

The second quarter opened with OJ going off left tackle and fumbling the football, which was recovered by Gary junior Jerry

Grecco. Indiana in the next series of downs, completed two passes one from Gonso to Butcher, the other from Gonso to Gage. The Hoosiers however, could not sustain their drive, and USC took over on downs.

After an exchange of punts Indiana would get a return from Gonso to the 35. Indiana readied itself for another drive with the score still in favor of Southern Cal 7 to 0, and the Hoosiers still very much in the game. The first snap from center saw a hand off from Gonso to Isenbarger for a 3 yard gain. Cole took the ball and carried up the middle for an 8 yard gain, and a first down on the USC 24. Indiana was presented with its greatest scoring opportunity yet. Mike Krivoshia ran off left tackle for no gain. Gonso rolled out, and Indiana returned to the air, as Gonso hit Butcher with a pass that carried the Hoosiers all the way to the USC 9. A Cole dive across the middle for 2, and Indiana was down to the USC 7. Gonso then rolled to his left and found tightend Al Gage who had come up with so many big catches throughout the season in the end zone. Gage could not hang on to the football, and Indiana faced third and 7. Gonso ran the ball himself on a quarterback keeper off left tackle, only to be stopped at the 10 for a loss on the play. Dave Kornowa would come in to attempt to put the Hoosiers on the scoreboard with a 27 yard field goal, and with 6:57 to go in the second quarter IU trailed 7 to 3.

USC would take the kickoff at their own 15 and return the ball to the 27. Southern Cal then marched down the field in a 13 play drive ending at the Hoosier 10, on a catch by senior Ron Drake. USC needing to reach the 5 for a first down, had come up short.. The big defensive play for IU on the USC drive, was sacking Sogge on the twelfth play of the drive, at the Indiana 27, making it a fourth and 22.

IU unable to move the football punted the ball back to Southern Cal. USC would then try a desperation pass to the Indiana 5, only to have Nate Cunningham intercept the pass and run the ball out to the 33, before going down as the first half came to and end with Southern Cal leading 7 to 3. At the end of the first half, the Hoosier faithful would take heart in the fact that their Cardiac Kids were trailing only 7-3. The score seemed a small obstacle to overcome after experiencing this come from behind season.

Indiana University Archives

IU would start the second half out strong on defense with a three and out by the Trojans. Indiana took over at the 23 following a Gage return. Isenbarger ran a pitch from Gonso for a 14 yard gain out to the 37, for a first down. Isenbarger then ran up the middle for 3. At this point Indiana's offense stalled, and the Hoosiers were forced to punt. The Trojans took over on their own 33. Southern Cal would then take a 9 play drive to the 27 for a field goal attempt that was no good, and the score remained 7-3. Indiana's offense would again stall, and once more the Hoosiers would be forced to punt. The Trojans then put together another drive, and an 8 yard run by Simpson, followed by an Aldridge extra point, made the score 14 to 3.

There would be one very light hearted moment in the game, when Gonso's leg cramped up and backup Mike Perry came into the game. Perry, more then a little excited playing in such a big game, came into the Hoosier huddle and proceeded to call a play that the Hoosiers did not have. The players in the huddle told

Mike, we don't even have that play, what do you want us to do? Jade Butcher standing there just said "Hey Mike, throw me an out and I will get the ball. Well, Perry throws the ball, and its going, and going, and going until it hits a tuba player about 8 rows up in the stands. Jade came back in the huddle, and says Mike just calm down take a deep breath and get it near me, I will catch it." recalled Mauro. Driving late in the fourth quarter, the national broadcasters would say watch out for this Hoosier team, if they can score here and make it 14-10, then anything can happen, and these Cardiac Kids may just pull out another victory. The Hoosiers would then pull out a play put in to take advantage of Isenbarger's ability; a swing pass out of the backfield, down the sideline where he would be isolated on a linebacker. The play would be a true mismatch. As the play developed, everything went well except the linebacker was Adrain Young, an All-American who ran step for step with Isenbarger, and was able to knock the play down at the last minute. On the next play, Eric Stolberg was hurt coming across the middle for a pass, and the Hoosier threat ended. IU's first Bowl appearance ended in a 14 to 3 loss to number one USC.

The Trojans out gained IU on the day 317 yards to 189. USC would have 20 first downs to Indiana's 13, and Simpson would gain 128 yards scoring 2 touchdowns. Indiana fans were none the less, proud of these valiant warriors of Coach Pont. The Cardiac Kids, as they became known, had occupied a special place in the minds and hearts of their fans. This season would be a season to remember forever. The seniors would leave to pursue their careers. The juniors and sophomores would return for one or two more years respectively. The '68 Rose Bowl team would go on to become the first Indiana team to start an endowment fund of their own for the University. They would forever remain a family of teammates, honored by their adoring friends and fans. While it was their privilege to play at IU, it was far more the privilege of the thousands of fans of that fantastic season to watch them.

GAME STATISTICS	IU	USC
First Downs	13	20
Yards Rushing	79	248
Yards Passing	110	69
Total Offense	189	317
Passes	9-25-1	5-9-1
Punts	4-41	4-41
Fumbles/Lost	2-1	3-1
Penalties/Yards	4-29	8-65

INDIVIDUAL STATISTICS
RUSHING
IU

Isenbarger	12-38
Cole	10-21
Gonso	15-11
Krivoshia	4-9

USC

Simpson	25-128-2TDs
Scott	18-85
Sogge	6-17
Page	5-14
Dale	2-10
McCullough	1-(-6)

PASSING
IU
Gonso   25-9-110-0TD-1INT

USC

Sogge	7-4-57-0TD-1INT
Page	1-1-12-0-0
Simpson	1-0-0-0-0

RECEIVING

IU

Gage	6-67
Butcher	3-43

USC

Drake	3-46
McCullough	2-23

Chapter 17

Notes on the Season

This chapter is a collection of quotes by the coaches, players and sports writer Bob Hammel about the fantastic run by the '67 Indiana University football team. I am deeply indebted to each for sharing their time and experiences with me.

Harold Mauro recalled what made John Pont such a great coach, "The thing that really impressed us right away with John was we didn't have names on our helmets, yet on the first day of practice he called everyone of us by our names. That took some work, studying films, bios on individuals, that was a very impressive first impression. We said we have something here, let's work hard and see what we can do."

Harry Gonso after the Michigan game, "I remember just handing the ball to John every play and we went down and scored the winning touchdown."

Harold Mauro, "John recruited speed, real speed, and as an offensive lineman, you didn't have to hold your blocks as long."

Harold Mauro, "John Isenbarger used to say to us, he wore number 17, just give me 17 inches. We thought our line splits are just two feet, even if we got knocked down, we could give John 17 inches."

Harold Mauro in answering what made this team special, "One thing was that a new coach gave a lot of player's new life. I was playing linebacker most of the time under Dickens. When John came, I was switched to center because I was the punt snapper and I didn't play defense so that I would not get my hands banged up." Mauro continued to talk about how this team came together and what made this team so tough, "The old guys, some fifth year seniors like myself, Bob Russell, Rick Spickard, we as a line, just jelled and you have to be able to run the football in the Big Ten. If you can run and play a little defense, you can survive in this league. The 4-4 defense that we played, no one else played it in the league. Scout teams had to go from a 50 to a 44. This was really different for the scout teams. The reads are different, alignments are different, and keys are different. It was just hard for other teams to prepare for us. The defense had a lot of guys that made personal sacrifices; one was our Captain, Doug Crusan."

Ken Kaczmarek on why this team was so good, "John Pont was first class. Our assistant coaches were very good; they always had us really prepared. Our junior year, we could have easily won 5 or 6 games. We had the Miami game won, but the weather and a blocked punt cost us a victory that turned into a 7-6 loss." On the senior year, "Our team came together, we had skilled position players that were sophomores, and they really believed they were going to be good. The timing and putting together the classes just jelled. It all came together, even our trainers were awesome. They had us ready to play. Our linebackers we had could all play today. All were very fast. We could run on the first 3 yards, we were as quick as anyone. We had eight guys that could play the line and we had eight good linebackers; people that were smart and good athletes. Sniadecki, probably most consistent, Duffy, someone who would create a lot of activity, Marks and Moynihan were both steady and consistent, Gill, Price, do a lot of damage, not only quick and fast, but stronger. If Bob Kirk would have been able to play in The Rose Bowl, his quickness would have tied up Rossovich 3 or 4 plays, plays we could have won the game. They were faster, but we were quicker. We were doing a lot of blitzing. I was playing in the Hula Bowl. I was packing my stuff and we had to change my face mask because it was literally bent. What happened was they ran the I formation and whichever way they were coming, the linebacker was filling, and we were hitting head to head with the fullback. We hit so many times, the face mask was just bent. We hit them straight on so Simpson would have no where to go."

Doug Crusan on what made this team so special, "The synergy made us special. The senior class had played a lot of tough people, MSU, Michigan, and Purdue. We had a nice, solid, junior class and then we had the brashness of the sophomore class; and I mean that as a compliment. We just melded together as a family." Crusan talking about the weight reduction program said, "I came back that fall at 232. I had great stamina. I felt the fastest I had ever been. "

Crusan reflecting on moving from offense to defense, "After four games, I was still concerned about playing defense. I went to Coach Pont, and he said, alright this week you will practice with both the offense and defense, and we will decide before the game where you will play. Of course after the game, I said, ok, this defensive thing is alright."

Crusan's response upon being asked about the headlines the offense grabbed during the season, "Offense got the headlines? Wait a minute, you mean, and let's be distinctive here, it was the quarterback, running back, and wide receiver that got the headlines." Crusan's smile betrayed his feeling of love and admiration for his former teammates. "We were a very disciplined defense. We didn't go out of the bailiwick of what was established. If you do that you'll be very good, and we were."

Crusan on being the captain, "I hadn't thought about being the captain on the team, but it was a tremendous honor. I really appreciated all those who thought that I could do that."

Crusan describing the Arizona game, "They were after Jade because he was exciting and flamboyant. They were going to look for him. The first time he scored they saw him hold the ball above his head."

Isenbarger on Michigan State, "MSU does not lose a lot at home. They beat Michigan and Notre Dame up there. We went up there three straight years starting in '67, and beat them three years in a row. I got knocked out in the second quarter up there, but was able to come back. I had a pretty good run at Michigan that year."

Pont recalling the '67 season, "I always felt that we could do it, that we had something very special."

Pont remembering being up in the air on the People Mover at Disneyland with his wife, "It became a very peaceful time during that hectic two weeks."

Pont on assistant coach, Howard Brown who was the Hoosier link between the two great IU teams, the undefeated '45 team and The Rose Bowl Team, "Howard was one of the most positive people I have ever been around. We would be on a recruiting trip in Ohio or Illinois, and it would be cloudy or rainy, and Howard would say, ' Don't worry coach, the sun is shining back in Indiana' and he meant it."

Pont on taking the Indiana job, "I called Nixon after the offer from IU came to me, and he said you have to take it. You have to take the challenge, and that is what Indiana is offering you, the challenge. You could take the security you have at Yale, and it will be fine for the rest of your life, but the opportunity to raise the level of play at Indiana University, you have to accept that position."

Jade Butcher on Harry, "After practice, Harry and I would spend time working out. I got to know his technique and he knew mine." This would of course be very important during the season as they connected on touchdown pass after touchdown pass.

Jade remembering the Purdue game, "We had just scored, and it was 13-7. We were going for 2. We practiced this, and I was to stay in the game if we went for 2. Well, Harry says to coach, let's go for two. I jog off the field, not knowing we're going for two. Harry rolls out, and I am not even in the game. I'm standing next to coach. Well, he is standing there with his coffee and tie. He turns around putting his hands on his hips, and yells,' Jade!' right in my face. That was all he had to say, I felt bad, that would have given us a cush."

Jade on going to the Rose Bowl, "Going to the Rose Bowl, you just can't almost describe how the folks, the people out there, treated us. The plane was all decorated up. The Air Force guys had this great big sign saying Go Hoosiers. "

Jade in talking about his experiences at IU, said that former basketball coach, Branch McCracken had befriended him when he first came to IU, "We would drink coffee and eat donuts together almost every morning. He was a great man. I could have played for him now."

Jade remembered when coming to Indiana, he was recruited for defense and a great thrill for him was that he got to play a little defense in the Purdue game.

Terry Cole told Bill James of the Chicago Daily News, "One thing I've learned here is that we've always had the talent here. Look at all the Indiana players that go into pro ranks, but we had absolutely no spirit. This year, we caught the spirit."

Jim Sniadecki said about Pont, "I am sold on him. Pont is

great. I wouldn't play for any other coach."

Mike Perry explained to Jack Schneider of the Courier-Journal and Times what it's like to play against Captain Doug Crusan, "Crusan is murder. You just can't get away from him. I never saw a guy so big who can move so fast, and when he hits you, you really get jarred."

Eric Stolberg explained to Schneider, "I don't know anyone on the team who doesn't like and respect Harry. He kids with the other players, especially with the linemen about their blocking, but when another player makes a good play, Harry always has a good word for them. He's not only a fine player, but he's also a very good leader on and off the field."

Pont talked about Cassells with Jack Schneider, "Cassells was injured in practice before our second game. For the shoulder to heal properly, he would have had to lay out for four or five weeks. We left it up to Gary, and he decided he wanted to go ahead and play with his shoulder taped up. Gary didn't do any hitting in practice before the last four games. This was to relieve the soreness. His willingness to play hurt has been true of some of our other players this year too. It's a good sign. The kids are willing to pay that little extra price that success demands."

Jade would remember getting the game ball his senior year against Michigan State for his 10 catches that day, which at the time was an Indiana record.

Gonso on Southern Cal, "They were big; they had five Terry Coles to our one. They were very, very big, just a better football team that day."

Gonso on Pont, "I love that guy."

Gonso on the Purdue game, "I just remember literally praying at the end of the game that the defense would hold."

Harold Mauro remembered, "A big thrill came as I was presented the game ball after defeating Kansas in our second game of the season."

In the categories of giving back, the '67 team, the Rose Bowl Team, established the first ever endowment at Indiana University by an athletic team. In talking with many players, they were as proud of this and their success in their lives as what they did on the gridiron.

Another example of the love this team has for each other was demonstrated by Harold Mauro. He found the mold for their Rose Bowl rings and had duplicates made for a couple of players that had lost theirs.

Mauro talking about one play in the Rose Bowl, "I did tackle O.J., he cut into me, and I just happened to be there and knocked him down, so I got credit for the tackle."

Bloomington sports writer, Bob Hammel, who traveled with the team all year, provided some interesting insights into the season. Hammel talked about the connection between the two Johns, Pont and Isenbarger. "You know Pont was the first freshman that Woody Hayes ever started. Pont in his very first game was returning a kick. He was back to return the kick when he dropped the ball. He proceeded to pick the ball up and return it 96 yards for a touchdown. Afterward, Pont said 'I dropped the ball because I played for Woody Hayes and I picked it up and scored because I played for Woody Hayes.' In much the same way, John Isenbarger in the Michigan game ran rather than punt because he played for John Pont and he ran the ball back almost the entire 80 yards for a touchdown because he played for John Pont."

Pont, who turned 40 during the season, was asked by a writer what he thought about this storybook season. Pont's response was "I wish I had the book so I could read the next chapter."

Hammel thought that, "Pont identified with the sophomores because he had been such a good young player himself. He had an appreciation for what a young player goes through. He came up with that Miami of Ohio discipline but he let those guys be themselves. He let Jade hoist the ball going into the end zone."

Hammel on Russell, "He was a medical student that gave up medical school for one year to come back and play. Little did he know that he would wind up playing in the Rose Bowl."

Hammel on the team "I don't know if they would have been as good for any other coach, their pluses came out and their minuses were not a problem."

Hammel on the Michigan game "A few years later we were at Michigan and the AD was talking about the '67 game. He was talking about the missed field goal late in the game by Michigan to keep the score tied at 20 to 20. We were at this press party and he said, 'Watch this film. Watch this guy, watch this guy kick. He kicks it so low that he kicks his own center in the butt. Indiana didn't block it he just kicks his own man in the butt.' "

Hammel on Crusan, "Enormous sacrifice by Crusan. Doug was a clear pro prospect as an offensive lineman. For him to go to the defense jeopardized that. Plus he had to lose all that weight, all those things he just did for the team. The amazing thing is that he did it so willingly and he became a defensive player. He was drafted as an offensive lineman so it didn't hurt him any. I think the feeling was look at what this kid has done you can't get any better attitude than that."

Hammel on Isenbarger, "John was an outstanding basketball player and pole vaulter in track in high school. If Pont had made him the quarterback he would have been great; just as Gonso would have been a great tailback."

Hammel on Kirk, "I really felt sorry for Bob Kirk. He had an outstanding season and to get hurt and miss playing in the Rose Bowl you just had to feel sorry for him. They weren't sure who to replace him with until the day before the game."

The '67 team became the first and only football team in university history to win the Big Ten Championship and go to the Rose Bowl. Indiana would also become the first team in university history to win all three trophy games in the same season. Indiana captured the Bourbon Barrel over Kentucky 12 to 10. They won the Brass Spittoon 14 to 13 over Michigan State, and they defeated Purdue to win the Old Oaken Bucket 19 to 14.

Chapter 18

Terry Cole
"T-Bear"

Terry Cole was a legend at Mitchell High School in south central Indiana. As a senior, Terry set a new state record scoring 186 points in 8 games. He also gained 1,339 yards in 131 carries scoring 25 touchdowns as he led Mitchell to an undefeated 8 and 0 season. Terry's junior year, he had led Mitchell to a 7-1 record and in his career, he would score 411 points while gaining 3000 yards. In one game, Terry scored all 63 of Mitchell's points as they won 63 to 0.

Indiana University Archives
(966-0228.6)

Indiana recruited Terry Cole heavily. The recruitment was led by Coach Phil Dickens and Ted Smith, a former captain of the '59-60 Hoosier football team. These two persuaded Terry to choose Indiana over Kentucky. In his first season, Terry would be named the most valuable player as a back on his freshman team. In 1965, Terry would lead IU in rushing with 286 yards and 2 touchdowns. His senior year, he sacrificed carried to become a blocking back on the '67 team that went to the Rose Bowl. Terry however was not without glory moments that season. In his final home game, he led Indiana to a victory in the Old Oaken Bucket game, rushing for 155 yards on 15 carries and a touchdown. He was selected AP Back of the Week for his performance.

Following graduation, he was drafted by the Baltimore Colts in 1968. He went on to become the Colts Rookie of the Year and NFL runner-up to their Rookie of the Year honors. Terry would be on the Colts Super Bowl III Team. He would play for the Pittsburg Steelers in 1970. Terry would then play for the Dolphins in 1971 and '72 playing for the undefeated Superbowl Champs, the Miami Dolphins. In 1986, Terry founded Cole-Chem Corporation based in both Indiana and California. Terry would be inducted into the Indiana Football Hall of Fame in 1992.

Stories about Terry were many and as his friend, Doug Crusan, would say, "most will go to the grave with me." But it was very clear in talking with the players how important Terry had been in their lives both during the '67 season and after. Pont would say about Cole during his time at IU and especially during the '67 season that Terry did a beautiful job of straight ahead running to help keep the defense honest. He would go on to say that Terry's assignment on the outside was to get the defensive end down. He would perform that task very well all season. Terry would give of himself to do what he could to help the team win and win they would in 1968.

Terry's friend, Jade Butcher, would recall, "Terry was a Big Red connoisseur. He was always saying let's go to Bedford and get some Big Red." So they would get in the car and drive to Bedford in Lawrence County to get a Big Red soda since Bloomington's Monroe County didn't carry any.

Terry Cole received the 2005 Z.G. Clevenger Award. On November 11, 2005 Terry would become the second member of the "67 team to pass away. Terry presence is still greatly missed by his friends on the team and those fans of this football team. Terry was truly a special member of the team as he was one of many who gave of themselves in order that this team could do the impossible.

Chapter 19

Doug Crusan
"The Captain"

Indiana University Archives
(966-0248.9)

Crusan was the third player from Monessen, Pennsylvania to be recruited by Phil Dickens to play at Indiana University during the '60s. All three of these players lived within 2 blocks of one another. One player, Bill Malinchak, starred at IU as a wide receiver only to have his records broken by Crusan's Rose Bowl teammate, Jade Butcher. Doug recalled, "The Big Ten came into Western Pennsylvania quite a bit. At Indiana, everyone was treated fairly. It was a great university, with great people, and that word carried." Doug was named the Most Valuable Lineman on his freshmen team at IU. He started his sophomore and junior year on the offensive line.

In the spring of Crusan's junior year, he was approached by Coach Pont who wanted two things of Doug; one was for Doug to switch from offense to defense. He also wanted Doug to lose between 35 and 40 pounds for the coming season. Crusan would go back to Pennsylvania during the summer to work in the steel mills. Doug would report in the fall 35 pounds lighter. In his senior year, Doug would indeed move from offense to defense. He would become one of four players on Indiana's Rose Bowl Team to be named as an All-American in 1967. Crusan became the first defensive lineman in Indiana University history to be recognized as an All-American when he earned second team honors in the '67 season.

In 1967, Crusan would be named the team captain and help lead Indiana to their second Big Ten Championship and first ever Rose Bowl appearance. Crusan, during his senior season, had 76 tackles including 3 for losses, 2 broken up passes, and 3 fumble recoveries. Two of these fumble recoveries occurred during the Michigan game for which he was named Midwest Lineman of the Week. Following Crusan's senior season, he was selected to play in both the Senior Bowl and the All-American Bowl

Crusan became the second first-round draft choice of the Miami Dolphins in 1968. He would later say tongue and cheek, "My name was the household one, everyone knew me. The other number one pick was some guy named Larry Csonka." Doug would play offensive tackle for the Miami Dolphins from 1968 to 1974. During this time, he played in three Super Bowls, and was a member of the Dolphins Super Bowl Seven and Super Bowl Eight Championship Teams. His 1972 Championship Team was the only undefeated team in NFL history. Doug would also play in the longest NFL game in history. On December 25, 1971, the Dolphins played the Chiefs for 82 minutes and 45 seconds, in what would amount to five and one half quarters. This game would not only be the longest game in NFL history, but the last played in the Chiefs old stadium. In 1972, Doug's Dolphins would open in Kansas City's new Arrowhead Stadium.

Doug was elected to the Indiana University Hall of Fame in 1987 and to the Indiana Football Hall of Fame in 2007.

Chapter 20

Harry Gonso
"The Field General"

The decision had to be made if Harry was going to go to the Big Ten to play football, would he go to East Lansing and become a Michigan State Spartan, or would he go to Bloomington and become a Hoosier? According to Harry, who was an excellent baseball player and swimmer in high school, he wanted to see if he was good enough to play football in the Big Ten. Harry was indeed an excellent swimmer, in fact, he was one of the nation's best. He was clocked at a time of 22.5 seconds in the 50 yard freestyle. He also won the Ohio Diving Title for 15 and 16 year olds, and competed in track as well. The decision still remained and Harry said that he really liked Indiana and the coaching staff. Harry

Indiana University Archives (967-0099)

went on to say that Michigan State was number 1 in the nation and he wasn't sure if he was good enough to play for the Spartans. Harry would choose Indiana, and oh how glad Hoosier fans would be for that decision.

Harry's freshman year, the Hoosiers would go 1-1, defeating the Ohio State Buckeyes and losing to the Michigan State Spartans. His sophomore year, Gonso would be the Most Valuable Player on the IU team that played Southern California in the Rose Bowl. He completed 67 of 143 passes for 931 yards and nine touchdowns. He was also selected as an All Big Ten player. Gonso's junior year, he passed for 1,109 yards and 12 touchdown passes while winning his second consecutive MVP Honors for Indiana. Gonso finished his senior year throwing for 1,336 yards and 11 touchdowns.

While Harry was excelling on the field, he was duplicating that success in the classroom. He was Indiana's Second Academic All American selection as a sophomore in 1967. He earned Academic All Big Ten Honors following both his junior and senior years. He also received the prestigious Hoosier Award during his time. Upon completion of his playing career at IU, Gonso would enter law school at IU in Bloomington in 1970. He graduated in 1973 with honors. Gonso served as an IU Trustee for 18 years from 1976 to 1994. In 2005, Harry would leave his law practice to serve as Governor Daniels "Chief of Staff" for two years, before returning to Ice Miller to lead its Life Science practice.

Harry became a member of the original class of the Indiana Hall of Fame in 1982. Gonso was selected to the Indiana Football Hall of Fame in 2007.

As for his question of whether he was good enough to play at Michigan State, Gonso's Hoosiers played at Michigan State his sophomore, junior, and senior years. In all of these games, Indiana defeated MSU; question answered.

Chapter 21

Jade Butcher
"The Knothole Kid"

There was Jade Butcher hoisting the football high above his head with yet another key catch during that '67 Big Ten Championship, Rose bowl season. This is the picture most people remember when thinking of the Bloomington native. Butcher who stayed home to perform football heroics for the Indiana Hoosiers was himself a knothole kid, meeting his friends on Saturday mornings to go the football stadium to watch the Hoosiers play.

Jade a local high school hero was not a hard sale when it came time for Pont to convince the Bloomington kid to apply his skills for Indiana University.

Courtesy: IU Athletic Department (967-0120)

One of Jade best friends was the son of Indiana legend Howard Brown, who also happened to be the Hoosiers freshman coach. Jade who had enjoyed an outstanding high school career would in fact stay at home to play football.

Jade was recruited as much for his defense as for his offense. Jade led Bloomington High School with 13 pass interceptions and as Jade put it, "I really like to hit people instead of being hit." In Jades senior season, Evansville North beat Bloomington 7 to 0 to end their 17 game win streak.

Jade and Harry Gonso, as freshman, hooked up for a touchdown pass in each of their only two games against both Michigan State and Ohio State. This streak would continue for 4 more games into their sophomore season. Jade went on to be selected as a first team All Big Ten player in both his junior and senior years. He earned All American status in his senior year. In his final season at IU Jade caught 37 passes for a total of 552 yards and 10 touchdowns. Jade was a model of consistency, catching 10 touchdown passes in his sophomore, junior, and senior years. After his senior season, Jade would play in the North-South Game and the Hula Bowl.

Jade would end his career at IU holding records for passes received at 119, reception yardage at 1,919 yards, touchdowns at 30, and points with 180 total. His 30 career touchdown catches would remain a Big Ten record in 30 games and would stand until broken by Anthony Carter in 44 games. Harold Mauro would say of Jade "He had the unique ability of running great routes, anything within 5 yards of him he would catch. It was unbelievable! He was the greatest receiver that ever played in this league. I tell you, it took Anthony Carter 44 games and 4 bowl games to break his record."

John Isenbarger would say that Jade, "Would just go down field like he was going to block on the safety, then he would just turn up field and I would hit him with the halfback option pass."

Jade would go on to be drafted by the Falcons and last two weeks before being cut by the head coach Norm Van Brocklin. "I had long hair and white shoes just like Joe Namath and Coach Van Broklin didn't care for that."

Jade played for Memphis in the WFL, although an injury cut his career short. One of Jades good friends would use his name in his movie called Hoosiers as the character known as Ray Butcher. Jade played a small part in the movie.

Jade was elected to the IU Hall of Fame in 1988 and to the Indiana Football Hall of Fame in 2007. Jade set a standard by which all future wide receivers would be judged.

Chapter 22

Harold Mauro
"The Monk"

Indiana almost lost out on an outstanding leader, Harold Mauro, one of many Pennsylvania players recruited to come to Indiana during the '60's. . Harold originally committed to play for Bear Bryant at Alabama. The Crimson Tide lost out to the Cream and Crimson as Mauro's father gently told him the only player from the north to succeed at Alabama was Joe Namath, and you're not Joe Namath. Harold said the players already at IU told him they were getting something started here after the NCAA sanctions were lifted.

Mauro played linebacker on the 1964 and 1965 Indiana teams before misfortune

Indiana University Archives
(964-0160)

turned into a great blessing. Harold was moved from linebacker to center prior to the 1966 season before being injured and missing the '66 season. The blessing for both IU and Mauro was he became the starting center for IU's '67 team that would go to the Rose Bowl. Harold played a big part in the success of the '67 team, earning the game ball after the Kansas game.

Mauro earned his Bachelor's Degree in Physical Education in 1968. He served as an Indiana graduate assistant in 1968, and as an assistant coach for University High School in Bloomington for the

1969 and '70 school years. Harold returned to IU as an assistant freshman coach in 1971 and became a member of the varsity staff in 1972. He followed Coach Pont to Northwestern in 1973 before returning to IU in 1977 as the guards and centers coach. In 1982, he became the offensive coordinator. The next 22 years Harold served as the Senior Associate Athletic Director at Indiana. He would also become Director of Football Operations.

Mauro has been a part of every bowl game in IU football history. In addition to the 1967 Rose Bowl Team, Mauro was an assistant coach on Indiana's 1979 Holiday Bowl Championship squad, and was an administrator for the 1986 All-American Bowl, 1988 Peach Bowl, 1988 Liberty Bowl, 1990 Beach Bowl, 1991 Copper Bowl and the 1993 Independence Bowl teams. Harold was inducted into the Indiana Football Hall of Fame in 2007.

Chapter 23

Ken Kaczmarek
"Kaz"

Ken Kaczmarek, when asked why he chose IU, said, "There were three or four things; one was that I grew up in South Bend. Our coaches were really good at helping us select a college that was the right fit for us; schools that were the right fit both academically and places where we could play somewhere. We looked at three or

Courtesy: IU Athletic Department (966-0240)

four in the Big Ten, looking at their rosters. We looked at both the guards and the linebackers, so that I could play as a sophomore. I also looked at their business school, and thirdly, I loved the campus. They also told me they would help me if I wanted to go to grad school. I also saw that they were scheduled to play at Texas and Miami. For a boy from Indiana, that sounded exciting." Kaczmarek, who played at South Bend Saint Joseph, helped his team to a 23 win, 4 loss, and 2 tie record in his 3 years. He would be named All City, All County, and All State.

Kaczmarek started his career in 1964 under Coach Phil Dickens, and then played for Coach Pont his final years at Indiana. He was named to the First Team All Big Ten and All American his senior year. During Ken's senior year, he and Harold Dunn caused the fumble to help defeat Purdue 19-14. After his senior year, Ken played in the Hula Bowl.

Kaczmarek was drafted by the Minnesota Vikings, and would play two years with them. Following his professional career, Ken returned to Bloomington to work with Elliott and Associates. Kaczmarek was elected to the Indiana Football Hall of Fame in 2003.

Chapter 24

John Isenbarger
"The Cardiac Kid"

John was an All State football player for two years at Muncie Central. He was also an excellent basketball player and star pole vaulter in track for the Bearcats. John came to IU to play quarterback in football and play basketball for Coach Lou Watson. During the fall of his sophomore year, he waged a battle with Harry Gonso for the starting quarterback spot.

With 10 days to go before Indiana's first game, Coach Pont called John in to talk to him about the race for quarterback. Pont would say that I have to have you both playing, so I'm going to move you to tailback. Isenbarger asked why he was the one

Courtesy: IU Athletic Department (967-0126)

being moved, and Pont responded that he was bigger and he felt he would make the better tailback. Isenbarger, though disappointed, agreed to the move with some reservation since there were only 10 days left before the first game and he had never played tailback before. Pont would then go on to explain that he would still have the opportunity to pass in the offensive scheme on the halfback option play.

John would go on to lead Indiana in rushing for the '67 year with 579 yards on 120 carries with a 4.8 average and 4 rushing touchdowns. He threw 3 touchdown passes and caught 6 passes with one touchdown reception. He led the Big Ten in punting with a 38.8 average. John would go on to lead IU in rushing for 3 straight years while compiling 14 rushing touchdowns. His senior year, he rushed for 1,217 yards, an IU record at the time. Isenbarger was IU's Most Valuable Player in 1969 while earning All-American honors in '67 and '69. He earned first team All Big Ten in 1969. He played in the Hula Bowl, Coaches All-American Game, East-West Game, and the College All-Star Game in Chicago.

John was drafted by the San Francisco 49ers in 1970 and played for the 49ers four years, including three play-off years. For two of those years, he would average over 19 yards a catch. In 1974, he played for Hawaii in the World Football League. John was elected to the Indiana Football Hall of Fame in 1993 and the Indiana Hall of Fame in 1991.

Chapter 25

John Pont
"Coach"

Courtesy: IU and Harold Mauro

The first time Pont carried the ball for his Miami University football team, he went 96 yards for a touchdown. The Miami halfback did not stop until he set school records for touchdowns scored at 28, yards gained at 2,390, and most yards gained on kickoff returns with 874. His jersey, number 42, would be the first retired in school history. After college, he played professional football in Canada with Toronto.

Pont returned to Miami and became the freshman coach under Ara Parseghian. In 1956 when Parseghian moved on to Northwestern, John Pont became the Miami head coach. Pont's l957 and '58 squads won Mid-American Championships. In his seven years at Miami, his teams compiled a 43-22-1 record. Pont and his staff then set off for Yale University and in his two years at Yale, before coming to Indiana, his record was 12-5-1. In February of 1965, Pont was named the new head coach at Indiana University, succeeding Phil Dickens who resigned on December 22, 1964.

His first two seasons were not as successful as he hoped. The first season in 1965, IU was 2 and 8. In 1966 IU was 1-8-1, losing several close games. Pont turned the IU program around in 1967 going 9 and 2, winning the Big Ten Championship and going to the Rose Bowl. Pont was rewarded for his success, winning the Walter Camp Coach of the Year Award and the Bear Bryant Award. Pont would coach the sophomores of '67 to a three year record of 19 and 10.

Coach Pont's tenure at Indiana lasted 8 years before he left Indiana for Northwestern for 5 years. Pont would become involved with Japanese football, both coaching in Japan and hosting, along with the late Terry Hoeppner, Japanese coaches and players for clinics in America.

After taking Indiana to the Rose Bowl, Coach Pont received a phone call from President Nixon. The President offered Pont the job as director of the Selective Service. Coach Pont would go through normal back ground checks with the FBI. While the Ponts were in Hawaii for the Hula Bowl in January, they were waiting for a table for breakfast "when we get a phone call from the White House at the front desk. It had a pronounced affect because we never waited in line after that day again. We were seated now and that is the power of the White House." Pont said that he asked what would happen to him as director since they were phasing out the Selective Service. He was told that we will get you a job with any corporation in America; anywhere you want to go. Pont said he really just wanted to coach, so he decided to stay at Indiana. "I had told the sophomores that I would stay at IU for 4 years so I turned down the president, but I kept my promise to the players, which I think is very important."

John Pont received many honors during his playing and coaching career. He was named Miami's MVP in 1951, selected all MAC in '49, '50 and '51 while being honorable mention All-American in 1949. He was inducted into the Indiana Football Hall Of Fame in 1984.

Chapter 26

Players of '67

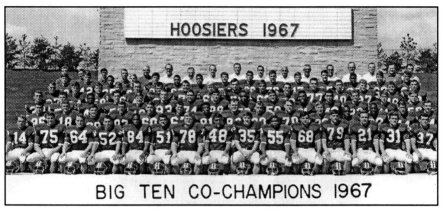

HOOSIERS 1967

BIG TEN CO-CHAMPIONS 1967

Indiana University Archives

Left to right, Row 1: Dave Kornowa, Doug Rhodus, Bob Russell, Brown Marks, Ken Kaczmarek, Harold Mauro, Doug Crusan, Terry Cole, Mike Krivshia, Cordell Gill, Gary Cassells, Rich Spickard, Gary Nichols, Bill Huff, Kevin Duffy, Row 2: Bill McCaa, Mike Perry, Bob Moynihan, Al Kamradt, Jerry Grecco, Pat Egan, Al Gage, John Carlson, Tom Bilunas, Bill Bergman, Dave Evans, Cal Wilson, Nate Cunningham, Roger Grove, Bob Douglas, Row 3: Mike Baughman, Steve Applegate, Mike Adams, Gayle Robinson, George Wortley, Jim Sniadecki, Al Schmidt, Bob Long, Bob Kirk, Mike Roth, Cal Snowden, Dick Waltz, Ken Long, Bill Ciz, Bill Bordner, Row 4: Bill Wolfe, Dave Hoehn, Steve Gruber, Harry Gonso, Mike Deal, Bob Nichols, Don Ghrist, Bob Geers, Harold Dunn, Don DeSalle, Tom DeMarco, John David, Jade Butcher, Dick Bozicevich, Frank Canarecci, Jay Mathias, Row 5: Tom Warriner, Don Warner, Greg Thaxton, Eric Stolberg, Bill Simon, Clarence Price, Ben Norman, Karl Pankratz, Bill Paulus, Ed Harrison, John Isenbarger, Walt Jurkiewicz, Charlie Murphy, E.G. White, Fred Mitchell Row 6: Managers John Rabold, Mike Dumke, Blondie Levy, and Equipment Manager Red Grow, Head Trainer Warren Ariail, Assistant Trainers Ted Verliahay, and Steve Moore, Head Coach John Pont, Assistant Coaches Charley McDaniel, Howard Brown, Jake VanSchoyck, Herb Fairfield, Jay Fry, Ernie Plank, Nick Mourouzis, and Bob Hicks,. Cheerleaders Walt Berg, Peggy Kellum, Ron Corley, Dick Salib, Ned Beach, Pat Kivland, Dave Keiler, Wendy Franey, Connie Clark, Captain Debbie White, Marabeth Wells, Cindy Skidmore

Gary Cassells

Cassells was from West Hartford, Connecticut. Gary was an outstanding football and basketball player at Conrad High School. Gary started just a few games his junior year in 1966. As a senior, he earned first team All American and All Big Ten honors as part of Indiana's Rose Bowl Team.

Bob Russell

Russell, a senior from Mansfield, Ohio, like Gary Cassells, came to IU under Coach Phil Dickens. Russell became one of the outstanding offensive lineman on the team. In 1967 Russell earned an 80% blocking rating for the entire season.

Rick Spickard

Spickard, a junior from Highland High School started in 1965, but sat out the '66 season with injuries. He recovered an Isenbarger fumble in the end zone against Illinois for IU's first score in Indiana's 20 to7 victory; the third win of the season. He would grade out the year in '67 with a 74% blocking rating. Spickard played in both the North-South Game and the American Games.

Bob Kirk

Kirk, a junior from Bloomington University High, was an outstanding lineman for the '67 team after starting his career as a split end. He earned All State honors at University High. His injury before the Rose Bowl game was very costly to the Hoosiers.

Mike Krivoshia

Krivoshia was a senior from Midland, Pennsylvania. He would lead Indiana in rushing for the '66 season with 675 yards for a 3.8 average. He was an All State and All American at Lincoln High School. In 1967, he rushed for 290 yards and 3 touchdowns.

Al Gage

Gage, a junior from East St. Louis, Illinois, was an outstanding tight end for the '67 Hoosiers. He caught 21 passes on the year for 343 yards and 1 touchdown, that one being the game winner in the opener against Kentucky. His 6 catches in the Rose Bowl were the most in the game. For the season, he had a 79% blocking proficiency rating.

Eric Stolberg
Stolberg was a sophomore from Cuyahoga Falls, Ohio. He was an All District halfback in high school. He played 187 minutes for the '67 champs, catching 5 passes for 73 yards and one touchdown. Stolberg played in the East West Shrine Game.

Ben Norman
Norman was a sophomore from Jacksonville, Florida. He would catch 3 passes on the year for 45 yards for a 15 yards per catch average.

Al Kamradt
Kamradt, a junior from Taft High School in Chicago, caught two passes on the year for 22 yards and an eleven yard per catch average.

Mike Perry
Perry was a junior from Broad Ripple High School in Indianapolis. This Ripple Rocket completed 5 passes in 9 attempts for 157 yards and a touchdown on the season. He also rushed for 51 yards and two 2 point conversions in the Arizona game.

Bill Wolfe
Wolfe was a sophomore from Decatur Illinois where he was an All State player in football while also staring in basketball and track. He made 3 solo tackles in the Illinois game. Wolfe was named the outstanding player in the Wisconsin game with 11 tackles.

Kevin Duffy
Duffy was a senior from Wethersfield High School in Connecticut. Duffy, playing on the offensive side in high school, set a school rushing record. He started for the Hoosiers in 1966. Duffy, who played linebacker for the Hoosiers, intercepted two passes and made 7 tackles in the Michigan State game.

Dave Kornowa

Kornowa from Toledo, Ohio, lettered in football, basketball, and baseball at Woodward High School. He came to IU as a quarterback an earned the number one back up spot in 1966. In 1967, he had 3 interceptions. Kornowa is best known for his game winning field goal against Kansas and his field goal against USC in the Rose Bowl that produced IU's only score in the game.

Jim Sniadecki

Sniadecki, a junior from South Bend St.Joseph, followed teammate Ken Kaczmarek to IU and Hoosiers were delighted with his choice. Sniadecki led the '66 team and the Big Ten in tackles for loss with 12 for 53 yards. In 1967, he took part in 84 tackles, 59 of them solo tackles. Jim earned second team All American honors in 1968. He played in the East West Shrine Game and the Hula Bowl. He was the forth round pick of the San Francisco 49ers where he would play from 1969 to 1973.

Cal Snowden

Snowden, a junior from Washington D. C., was All Metropolitan and a Prep All-American at Roosevelt High School. In 1967, Cal recorded 54 tackles and lead the team in tackles for loss with 10 for a total of 47 yards. Snowden would be selected second team All Big Ten.

Brown Marks

Marks was a 6-3 senior from Magnolia, Mississippi. In 1967, he had 71 tackles with one fumble recovery.

Tom Bilunas

Bilunas, a junior from Gary Andrean, was an All State player in high school. Tom, in 1967, would record 43 tackles, 27 of them solos. He was also second on the Hoosiers with 5 broken up passes. Bilunas became an Academic All Big Ten.

Nate Cunningham

Cunningham was a 6-1 junior from Danville, Illinois. He was a co-leader in interceptions for the ' 67 Hoosiers with 3. He returned an interception in the Arizona game for a 55 yard touchdown. Nate also made 58 tackles in '67, 44 of them solos. Cunningham would play in the East West Shrine Game.

Mike Deal
Deal was a sophomore from Hobart on the '67 team. His father was a star on the '45 undefeated Indiana team and his brother would play for the '79 Holiday Bowl team. Mike played in the Blue-Gray Bowl and the Senior Bowl.

Mike Baughman
Baughman was a 6-4 sophomore from Lancaster, Ohio. He recorded 45 tackles, intercepted one pass while breaking up 5 others. Baughman will be remembered most for his recovery of a Perry Williams fumble on the four in the '67 Purdue game that gave IU a 19 to 14 victory in the bucket game.

Jerry Grecco
Grecco was a 6-1 junior from Gary Andrean. In the 67 season, Grecco recorded 35 tackles. He also recovered a USC fumble in the Rose Bowl.

Don Warner
Warner, like Grecco and Bilunas, was from Gary Andrean. He shared IU kicking duties with Isenbarger and Kornowa. Warner's 11 extra points on the season ranked him as IU's sixth leading scorer for 1967.

Harold Dunn
Dunn was a 6-4 sophomore from Mt. Sterling, Ohio. He recorded 7 tackles in the Purdue game, including teaming with Ken Kaczmarek on the famous Williams fumble. He also recovered one fumble in that game. Harold Dunn has passed away, but like Terry Cole, will never fade from our memory.

Chapter 27

Honors of the '67 Hoosiers

Coach John Pont would be honored at the end of the season with Coach of the Year awards by The Football Writers, The Sporting News, The American Football Coaches Association, The Cleveland Touchdown Club, and The Washington Touchdown Club. Indiana gained one first time All-American in offensive guard Gary Cassells, selected first team by the AP Football Writers and The Walter Camp Foundation. He was named to the second team All-American list by the UPI, and All Big Ten for both the AP and UPI. Sophomore quarterback Harry Gonso earned first team All Big Ten for the UPI and the second team All Big Ten for the AP. He was selected Honorable Mention All-American by the AP. Muncie tailback, John Isenbarger, would gather All-American Honors from the Football News and be an Honorable Mention All-American from the AP. John was selected second team All Big Ten by both the AP and UPI.

The team captain, defensive tackle, Doug Crusan, would be 2nd team All-American for the Central Press and an AP Honorable Mention All-American. Both the AP and UPI selected Doug as second team All Big Ten. Indiana's other offensive guard, Bob Russell, received Honorable Mention All-American status and second team All Big Ten from the AP.

Two of Indiana's linebackers would gather honors for the '67 season as well. Ken Kaczmarek received third team All-American for the Central Press, and an Honorable Mention All-American for the AP. Ken was selected first team All Big Ten by the AP. The other linebacker honored, Jim Sniadecki, was named Honorable Mention All-American by the AP, and first team All Big Ten by the same organization. Finally, defensive end, Cal Snowden, would receive Honorable Mention All-American honors from the AP, and also joined their second team All Big Ten group.

The Hoosiers would pass out their own honors among themselves, with Harry Gonso being named the team's Most Valuable Player. The Most Proficient Exterior Lineman Award would go to tight end Al Gage. Bob Russell would receive the Most-Proficient Interior Lineman Award, and the Most Proficient Back would be the senior from Mitchell, Indiana, Terry Cole. The Most Proficient Defensive Lineman Award was shared by Cal Showden and Tom Bilunas. The Most Proficient Linebacker was Jim Sniadecki, while senior Dave Kornowa would be named the Most Proficient Defensive Back. A final award would be justifiably shared 3 ways; as Butcher, Gonso, and Isenbarger split the honor of Sophomore of the Year.

Indiana saw the crowd in Bloomington increase, and as the season rolled along 42,311 would come to the Kentucky game, as many from southern Indiana and Kentucky made the drive up to Bloomington. Indiana would then see crowds of 34,861; 41,353; 46,910 and 52,770 for the Kansas, Iowa, Wisconsin, Purdue respectively, setting an attendance record of 218,205 for an average of 43,641 shattering the previous record of 169,484 and a 33,897 average. The largest crowd the Hoosiers would play before was 102,996 in the Rose Bowl.

Indiana would have many outstanding performances to accompany a truly outstanding season. The most rushing yards in a game belongs to senior Terry Cole in his last home game against Purdue with 155 yards. Indianapolis native and back up quarterback, Mike Perry, would pass for the most yards in a game with his performance in Arizona with 157 yards. MVP Harry Gonso set four marks against Kentucky with the most plays at 40, the most total offense at 236, the most passes completed with 11, and the best completion mark at .733. Bloomington native, Jade Butcher, set 5 marks with most catches in a game, 5 against Iowa, Kansas and Arizona. He would also have the most yards caught in a game with 175, the longest pass play and scoring play with 73 yards against Arizona. Jade shared with fellow sophomore John Isenbarger, the most points scored in a game with 12. John accomplished this feat at Ann Arbor against Michigan while Jade scored 12 in his big game against Arizona. Harry and Terry would share the longest run from scrimmage with 63 yard runs; Gonso in the first game of the season against Kentucky, and Cole in the last game of the season against Purdue. Nate Cunningham racked up the longest interception return, which would turn into a touchdown, as he raced 55 yards against Arizona on October 28th.

John Isenbarger in addition to sharing with Butcher the most points in a game, would also lead the Hoosiers in longest punt with 69 yards vs. Minnesota and longest kickoff return with his 33 yard return against Iowa that would start the drive for the winning score in IU's brilliant 21-17 come from behind victory over the Hawkeyes.

Bill Murphy

Author Bill Murphy has been an IU season ticket holder in football and basketball for decades, starting as a Knot Hole Kid in the late 1950s. The Cardiac Kids; A Season to Remember achieves his dream to write and share the story of the magical 1967 Indiana University football team and season.

Murphy teaches U.S. History at Harris Elementary School in Greenfield, Indiana as he has for nearly 30 years. Bill continues to coach basketball in the Greenfield system, a veteran of over 36 seasons and over 1,100 games from fifth grade to the high school level. He feels privileged to have worked with thousands of students over his many years of dedicated service.

Bill Murphy and his publisher, Pen and Publish Inc., are grateful to the members of the 1967 team and Indiana University for their gracious assistance. They have pledged a portion of the book's royalties to the '67 team's room in the new IU Hall of Champions in the North End Zone Facility under construction at Memorial Stadium.

Bibliography

Pete Rhoda, David Biancanrano, Jeff Keag, Indiana Football Yearbook Metropolitan Press Bloomington Indiana, 2005

Indiana University Review Kentucky September 23,1967

Indiana University Review Iowa October 14, 1967

Indiana University Review Wisconsin November 4, 1967

Indiana University Review Purdue November 25, 1967

Indiana Scene Magazine December 10, 1993

Rose Bowl Program 2004

Jon Stine "Ten years later the Champions remember" Indiana Athletic Review October 15, 1977

Bob Owens "Hoosier Ready for Kentucky" The Bloomington Tribune September 24, 1967

Owens " Gonso lead IU Nips Kentucky" The Bloomington Tribune September 26,1967

Owens "Hoosiers Seek 2-0 Mark against Kansas" The Bloomington Tribune September 29, 1967

Charles Boutlett "Indiana tops Kansas" Chicago Tribune October 1, 1967

Bruce Morrison "Hoosiers Stun Illini" Chicago Sun Times October 8, 1967

Bob Hammel "Hoosiers Upend Illinios for No.3" Bloomington Bedford Sunday Herald imes October 8, 1967

David Conden "4 in Row for Indiana "Chicago Tribune October 15,1967

Roy Damer "Indiana wins 5th in Row" Chicago Tribune October 22, 1967

Robert Markus "Indiana Routs Arizona, 42-7" Chicago Tribune October 29,1967

Hammel " Good Heavens A Romp" Bloomington Daily Herald-Telephone October 29, 1967

Jack Schneider "Injured Guards Play Inspires IU Team" Louisville Times October 30, 1967

Schneider "Crusan Equal to Nations Best" LOuisville Times October 31, 1967

Schneider " Harry Gonso; Indiana, Is Fun-Loving Guy" Louisville Times November 2, 1967

Owens "7-Come-11" Bloomington Tribune November 3, 1967

Edger Munzel "It's No. 7" Chicago Sun Times November 5, 1967

Markus "Indiana Wins No. 7" Chicago Tribune November 5, 1967

Jack Griffin "Never Quit Hoosiers Catch Spartans 14-13" Chicago Sun Times November 12, 1967

Owens "IU One Game From Rose Bowl" Bloomington Tribune November 12, 1967

Hammel "Rose Bowl Express Derailed" Bloomington Daily Herald Telephone November19, 1967